# TOWNSHEND

## A CAREER
## BIOGRAPHY

# TOWNSHEND

## A CAREER BIOGRAPHY

## Chris Charlesworth

**PROTEUS BOOKS**
LONDON/ NEW YORK

PROTEUS BOOKS is an imprint of
The Proteus Publishing Group

*United States*
PROTEUS PUBLISHING CO., INC.
9 West 57th Street, Suite 4503
New York, NY 10019
*distributed by:*
CHERRY LANE BOOKS CO., INC.
PO Box 430,
Port Chester, NY 10573

*United Kingdom*
PROTEUS BOOKS LIMITED
Bremar House,
Sale Place,
London W2 1PT

ISBN 0 86276 245 6 (p/b)
0 86276 246 4 (h/b)

First published in US 1984
First published in UK 1984

*Editor:* Mike Brecher
*Designed by:* Adrian Hodgkins
*Typeset by:* Wordsmith Limited
*Printed* in Great Britain by
Chanctonbury Press

# INTRODUCTION

It's been forty-five minutes since the support group left the stage, and out front we're impatient. There have been two false alarms and the re-appearance of yet another roadie inspires slow handclapping. Banks of speakers tower upwards like the Manhattan skyline and the silent drum kit, all gilt and flash, awaits its master. The house lights have dimmed and anticipation is at fever pitch. "Ladies and gentlemen, please welcome............"

*"If it screams for truth rather than help, if it commits itself with a courage it can't be sure it really has, if it stands up and admits something is wrong but doesn't insist on blood then it is rock 'n' roll."*

Up we jump in a contagious surge of anxious excitement. The band stagger on, find their sockets and issue a deafening, uncontrolled warning: T-W-O-I-N-G from the bass guitar, W-O-O-M-P W-O-O-M-P like the foghorn of an ocean liner; TA-TA-TA TA-TA-TA from the drums, DUB-A-DE DUB-A-DE DUM-DUM B-O-O-M, a mad, tumbling roll; K-E-R-R-A-N-G from the guitar, then again, louder, slicing through the wild applause like thunderclaps from an electric heaven. Then the din abruptly stops and the guitarist leaps high into the air, and when his feet touch the ground he plays with discipline, furious angry discipline, short sharp chords, a riff we all recognise, and the singer rocks backwards, throws his microphone into the air, and catches it, screaming for truth. "Got a feeling inside......."

*"I am not a leader, neither yours nor anybody else's. I'm a rock*

*musician, a mirror. You see yourself when you see The Who."*

Two minutes into the show and we stand on the seats, swaying together, holding onto eachother so as not to topple over and miss the action. A boy in front sees himself reflected in the mirror and spins his arm like a propeller, pausing at the top of each arc, jumping on his seat as he completes a circle before whipping back round again. The first song finishes in a babbling crescendo; no delay, no speeches, another sharp riff, another rumble from the drums, another roar of recognition. "You think we look pretty good together.........."

*"When I was a kid the guitar was all I had. I wasn't tough enough to be a member of the gang. Not good looking enough to be in with the birds. Not clever enough to make it at school. Not good enough with the feet for football. I was a fucking loser."*

The song is over and all around the aisles fill with fans who punch the air in joyous release, yelling the words, carried along like raving anarchists. We maintain our momentum *between* songs. The singer is talking, barely heard, a brief announcement, and then the fucking loser leaps again, the seven-stone weakling jack-knifing in the air, and soars towards centre stage; two fist smashing chords held together by the bassman's deep zing. Drums reappear, another riff takes shape. "I'm gonna raise a fuss, I'm gonna raise a holler.........."

*"I remember when we started a lot of people used to say, 'The only reason you're doing what you're doing – all that leaping about – is because you're on something'. Actually it's never been all that difficult, all that leaping about. If all you ever had to do over two hours is shuffle your feet every now and again, move backwards and forwards between a microphone and an amplifier and then do, say, ten drop kicks – well, I think in two hours you can manage that without getting a heart attack."*

So we all pause for a breather and a laugh, to let eachother know we're human after all. It's all a trick and we've been fooled again but the magician is enjoying himself and so are we. The drummer stands, announces his intention to sing. The crowd cheer, the singer feigns a pained expression and the guitarist blows a raspberry and then steps back, swaying slightly, plays a melodic arpeggio, and again we recognise the

8

tune; at first floating, ethereal, then stabbing, propulsive with a guitar solo that dips and dives like its author, carried along by the breeze, a tumbling descent of rhythm chords. "No-one knows what it's like to be the Sad man......."

*"You know it's really weird, but there have been whole tours which have taken place and I've been drunk from start to finish. But I can remember every second of every gig because there were little fragments where I got my body to work and the blood to flow. I was okay then."*

The choreography, casual yet crucial, is a sacrament; such a fine sight to see. They play as if a life depends on it and because of the pure undivided effort that goes into the performance we become drawn to the source and our blood starts to flow too. At times graceful, like a swan; at times clumsy, like a duckling, the guitarist glides around, his body working, carried like a surfer on the waves of sound. A song from the bassman. "My wife is coming after me............."

*"I think the thing really is that there's a certain honour attached to it because of the fact that rock has said, 'We will do it right. You've done it all wrong. We will show you that not only can we write a song like 'My Generation' where we write off the Establishment, where we write off the politicians, where we write off the group, but we write off the whole lot of you. We will get it right.'"*

The honourable music is heard now on a pre-recorded tape of synthesiser patterns, jangling, insistent, and as the song develops the patterns are framed with cannon fire. We salute each salvo and the guitarist gazes over teenage wasteland and pounds the stage like a clown. "Out here in the streets........."

*"Some kid writes to me and says, 'I've got all your records and I listen to your music all day long and I look at your pictures all the time and I write to you and all I get is a bleeding autographed picture. You don't know how much time I spend thinking about you.' I write back to him and say, 'You don't know how much time I spend thinking about teenagers.'"*

The guitarist is in a trance. Spinning like a top, he zigzags across stage, just missing a microphone stand, almost colliding with the singer and clearly out of control. When each bar finishes it is the cue for a gesture: an arm held high, a knee bend, a kick, a spin. These time-honoured jerks and jumps

9

belong to us and as the music becomes louder and more frenzied, gushing from speaker cabinets like the raging sea, audience and performers fuse together into one energy source, all powerful, momentarily indomitable. Now he stands before us, sweat pouring from his face. "Ever since I was a young boy..........."

*"I was very mystified by the fact that 'Tommy' was so financially successful. It was the first really good, well-intentioned thing that I'd ever done – the first time that I'd really wanted to do something good. And in a way, I suppose, I was trying to put out spiritual ideas, and then it embarrassed me that it had to make money. This is it – put on your Salvation Army uniform and your Rolls-Royce arrives in the post. Your place in heaven is guaranteed right here on earth."*

The momentum of the "opera" has intensified gradually for half an hour without pause under the direction of the Salvation Army captain. A bank of powerful white lights blaze outwards from the back of the stage and the whole scene is bathed in their glow. The finale emphasises the same spirit of unity that envelops us all, and we wave our arms madly as the pace quickens and the anthem-like climax pounds on remorselessly. "Listening to you.............."

*"When you've got an audience it is one of the most exhilarating experiences you can have, like dropping your trousers in front of people. It's the exhibitionist's delight. You want people to tear their hair out when you appear... you've really got to make them spew up."*

More synthesiser tapes fill the air, a march time, again identified by its fierce delivery, its defiant tone. Midway through the song there is a lull followed by an explosion and at the point of re-ignition the guitarist launches himself into the air and careers across stage from right to left, a fifty-foot flight, and lands on his knees and slides crazily into the wings. Appreciation spews forth. "There'll be fighting in the street....."

*"If I stood on stage worrying about the price of a guitar, then I'm not really playing music."*

The final song is not quite over. The bassman is still playing and the singer is dancing, smashing a tambourine against his microphone, stepping back to avoid the guitarist. Two tom-toms roll off the drum rostrum and a cymbal stand topples

10

with them. The guitarist's shoulder strap has come loose and he throws his instrument into the air, catches it and somehow continues playing. The noise is awesome, shapeless and climactic, a feast of feedback. Up goes the guitar again, only this time it is allowed to drop to the stage. Now he grips it by the neck and swings the weight around his head, then chops down as if using an axe, cleaving like a woodcutter: C-L-A-N-G and again, C-L-A-N-G, and the neck fractures, leaving the body attached by its strings alone. A signal, a crazy, distorted, hideous electric whine, continues to cry out, as if the guitar is in pain, crippled and keening. The guitarist gathers up the remains of his instrument, throws the heap of useless wood and wire into the air and, when its cries are finally reduced to a whimper, pushes over the line of speaker cabinets in a final orgy of absolute destruction.

*"Sometimes I really do believe that we're the only rock band on the face of the planet that knows what rock 'n' roll is all about."*

# CHAPTER ONE

It hurts like hell when you play the guitar for the first time. Clumsy fingertips sizzle and sting and blisters rise above soft skin like ugly warts on a skuller's palm. For the guitar to ring cleanly the strings must be pressed down firmly but the greater the pressure, the greater the pain, and when a carefully prepared chord is firmly struck yet sounds like a muffled fart, frustration drains away enthusiasm like a house of cards tumbling for the twenty-first time.

Pete tossed aside his guitar and inspected the white callouses on his left hand. His fingertips felt as though red hot needles had pierced the skin. He pulled a face, shook his wrist as if touched by a burning coal and stared down at the open page of a chord manual by his side. D seemed easy enough, E was a bit harder but A, with three fingers together across the second fret, was deceptively difficult. And as for F, with the first finger fretting two top strings at once, well that one... *that* one was an accomplishment somewhere in the realms of fantasy. Still, the simple G, with just one finger on the third fret of the first string, was no problem at all, didn't even sting much, and neither was the equally basic G7. So he picked up the guitar again and strummed gently, alternating G and G7, up and down, up and down, until the bounce in his right arm became a matter of routine, as steady as a metronome, as reliable as the ticking of his bedside clock.

Each time he made a downstroke he tapped his heel on the bedroom floor. And each time he tapped out this basic but monotonous rhythm the image of his secret ambition came more sharply into focus. The recurring daydream was a vision of sometime in the future when his skill on the guitar attracted widespread but reluctant acclaim from those who presently looked down upon him as a skinny little runt, a classroom joke. With the G chord still sounding and the pace of his right arm quickening in response to the ecstasy of imagination, girls swooned about him and men sought to be called his friend. It was a time when scores would be evened at last.

For reflected in the mirror of that bedroom in Ealing, the first rehearsal studio that Pete Townshend ever knew, was the body of a teenager that few could envy. Wafer thin arms with negligible biceps dangled loosely from bony shoulders and the contours of his rib cage formed a visible chevron against tight pale skin. Hip bones protruded beneath his hollow chest and matchstick legs tapered to the ground like jointed stilts. He appeared to himself to be a walking skeleton and while these unmanly features might be easily disguised beneath a school blazer and grey flannel trousers his face, with its unfortunate relief, was always and forever to be a blot on the landscape.

It was the one thing that caused more grief than the stinging pain in his fingers. It was his nose, a nose that rose majestically from beneath clear blue eyes and dominated his features as Mount Everest dominates the Himalayas. And like a mountain range it was craggy, rising to a narrow peak, neither bulbous nor round but sharp and pointed and when the sun caught him in profile a shadow descended from cheekbone to jaw.

To others of his year the snout became first a source of amusement and then cause for ridicule and, since its owner was not one to respond aggressively to these playground taunts, he bottled up the resentment inside his head until that day came when the dam would surely break.

"I'll bloody well show 'em," he vowed. "I'll push this huge hooter at them from every newspaper in England. Then they won't laugh at me."

And then the pain came back worse than before and again he saw his face in the mirror and repeated his vow; and so it went on until he found out for the first time just who he was and what he might become.

\* \* \* \* \*

Like the music that pained his fingertips, the nose that scarred his face was a family trait. It had been passed on from father to son without sympathy; seeming to Clifford Townshend a small price to pay for the contented and classless state his small family enjoyed. For Clifford Townshend did not look down his nose on those below nor look up to those above. Professional musicians mixed comfortably with rich and poor and high and low like all entertainers secure in their talent have done through the centuries.

The Townshend clan had made their home in West London for longer than Clifford could remember and their reluctance to ease into a specific social order fits snugly into a theory that somewhere down the line are aristocratic forebears. Townshends with an 'h' are outnumbered by the more common Townsends without an 'h' (by about twenty to one) but unfortunately there is no direct evidence to link this family with that of Marquis Townshend of Raynham Hall, Norfolk.

(According to the *Dictionary Of British Surnames* Townshend – or Townsend or Townend or Townen or Towsesend – indicates a 'dweller at the town's end' and was in evidence in England during the twelfth century in a variety of different spellings. The most celebrated Townshend, from whom the current Marquis is descended, is Charles "Turnip" Townshend (1673-1738), the Second Viscount, who was responsible for British foreign policy during the periods 1714-16 and 1721-30. On his retirement he devoted his life to the science of crop rotation with notable success, thus earning the soubriquet Turnip.)

Like his own son, Cliff was the son of a musician, Horace Arthur Townshend, born in 1882. (In turn the son of William Townshend who worked as a tailor's cutter in Chiswick during the mid-nineteenth century.) Horace was by day the manager and display specialist at a carpet warehouse and at other times a featured performer with the Jack Shepherd Concert Party who entertained holidaymakers during the summer months with

14

musical revues staged on the beaches and piers at Brighton. At Brentford Register Office on 5th February 1910, Horace married twenty-two-year-old Dorothy Blandford and they made their home together at 41, Whellock Road in the Turnham Green area of Chiswick.

Dorothy Blandford Townshend worked as an office clerk and shared with her husband the love of popular music that runs through this family like a freshwater stream. She took stage parts in the style known as soubrette; a fluttery maidservant or vain daughter in musical comedy, a role which required the implication of pertness, coquetry, romantic intrigue. Between them, Horace and Dorothy wrote comic songs and one of these joint compositions, a song called *Bathing In The Briny*, became a pre-war favourite on the piers of Southern England, a sheet music 'hit' of the day.

There are photographs of The Jack Shepherd Concert Review that show five men and three women in summery costumes; the girls in floral prints and the men with blazers, white pants and straw boaters. With a changing complement they performed in Brighton from the summer of 1903 until the Nineteen Thirties and Shepherd is best remembered as the man who gave a start to Max Miller, then Harry Sergeant, in the summer of 1919. For a period he called his troupe The Highwaymen, having adopted the stage name Shepherd after the famous highway robber. Shepherd thus became the first man to recognise a Townshend talent but he died in poor circumstances in Brighton in 1968, ten years after his protegé Horace Townshend.

In 1917, Horace and Dorothy produced a son they named Clifford Blandford and Cliff, as he came to be known, inherited their musical gifts to the extent that he would soon become the first in the Townshend line to make a fully professional career from popular music. He too was destined to pass these gifts on to *his* son and by this time the musical strain running through the Townshend blood had gained in strength: Betty Veronica Dennis, the girl he married, was a singer, the featured vocalist with a popular dance band, The Sidney Torch Orchestra.

Like the Townshends, the Dennis family was long established

15

in the British capital and an ambitious, independent streak ran through the family. Betty's father, Maurice Michael Dennis, born in 1902, lived in Hereford Street, Marylebone, and began his working life as the delivery driver for a local grocery business. He went on eventually to become the managing director of a similar enterprise and thereby followed in the footsteps of his own father, James William Dennis, who was a fishmonger by trade. At Marylebone Register Office on 23rd April, 1923, Maurice married Emma Elizabeth Hindley, the twenty-year-old daughter of a car mechanic called James William Hindley who lived nearby at 5, Little Church Street.

Their daughter Betty was born in 1924 and when Betty married Cliff Townshend at Pontypool Register Office on 16th April 1944, she falsified her age, adding two years on the wedding certificate. Cliff and Betty were serving in the wartime RAF, Cliff as Lance Corporal 923809 and Betty as WAAF Private 2203034, and they shared lodgings at 61, Tolley View in the village of Penygarn, close to their station in South Wales. Their first son, Peter Dennis Blandford was conceived at this address and named out of respect for his mother and paternal grandmother.

The boy who would one day play the guitar and exhibit his nose from every newspaper in England drew his first breath at the Central Middlesex Hospital Annexe in Chiswick on 19th May, 1945. Cliff and Betty had returned from South Wales to the area of Cliff's childhood, the same neighbourhood where they live to this day. They moved into a flat at 1b, Grosvenor Parade near Ealing Common and while Betty stayed home to tend their newly-born, Cliff resumed his career as a musician with tangible, if modest, success. The war was over; the country was at peace after five years and rejoicing in its freedom. A hot saxophonist who could play the newly-imported American swing music was unlikely to be out of work.

Cliff was thirteen when he put his lips to a mouthpiece for the first time. As a schoolboy he earned a modest living performing at bottle parties and by his twenties was accomplished on the alto clarinet, baritone and tenor saxophones. Before the outbreak of World War II he'd performed with three notable

16

dance bands – Ambrose, The Skyrockets and the Ted Heath Band – and worked as a session player in the recording studio backing aspiring singers. When war broke out, a number of noted dance band musicians, Cliff amongst them, joined the RAF together and became The Squadronaires, the most famous military dance band in Britain.

When hostilities ceased, The Squadronaires stayed together. Retaining their military title they performed one-nighters at dance halls up and down the country and at holiday camps during summer seasons. They broadcasted regularly for the BBC's Light Programme and until the emergence of Ted Heath's band in the fifties was the most popular dance band in Britain. At various times while Cliff played with them they were led by singer Jimmy Miller and, later, by pianist Ronnie Aldrich – their trombonist was a comical little chap, called George Chisholm who became famous for wiggling his moustache and wearing the uniform of a bowler-hatted gondolier. They made records for Decca, and Cliff made at least one recording in his own right, an instrumental tune called *Unchained Melody*, part of a film score by Alex North, which EMI's Columbia label released in 1955.

Betty Townshend, of independent spirit like her kin, continued her semi-professional career as a singer after her son was born and with either or both parents frequently away touring the country, the young heir to these musical gifts was often left in the care of his maternal grandmother Emma Dennis, now and forever to be affectionately known as Grandma Denny.

Clearly there was a Bohemian atmosphere in the comings and goings of this Ealing household, a belief that life was best enjoyed regardless, and the irregular life-style of his parents (Betty also managed an antique shop when she found time) communicated itself – and probably appealed – to their son. Children from nine-to-five households become subconsciously convinced that these habits will govern their own way of life but no such influence was transferred to Peter. Nine-to-five employment, so common to the majority of society, was quite foreign to him.

17

Pete gathered height under the watchful eye of Grandma Denny, played in the family's uncultivated garden and developed rather gracelessly into the tall, angular youth, whose mirrored reflection gave little pleasure to the eye. He attended Acton County Grammar School and sang in the school choir in a high nasal treble but his musical family saw no reason why this might develop into serious musical inclinations. There was no piano in the house, only his father's horns, and whatever artistic inclinations the boy displayed were limited to drawing, doodling cartoons, sketching with coloured crayons.

In the classroom he was well nigh invisible, self-conscious of his nose, a loner in the playground. Sometimes, to avoid the baiting that constantly threatened him, Pete escaped from the company of other eight-year-olds to a nearby rubbish tip where, from corrugated iron and scraps of discarded hardboard, he erected a tiny hut, a secret brooding ground. Here he fantasised about what life had in store. "I'll show them," he repeated to himself, kicking stones into the dirt.

Pete's twelfth summer was spent on the Isle Of Man where Cliff was engaged to play with The Squadronaires at the Butlins Holiday Camp. Many summers had been spent in this fashion but the lure of the beach, building sandcastles with a bucket and spade, had lost its appeal. As a diversion he was taken to see the film *Rock Around The Clock*, a star vehicle for Bill Haley, the kiss-curled singer who was at the vanguard of a new music craze imported from America.

To all intents and purposes *Rock Around The Clock*, the film, the song, the *phrase*, introduced this country to the most important development popular music has enjoyed in the twentieth century thus far, a type of music which, at its best, articulated emotions in a fashion infinitely more convincing than anything which had gone before. Most parents viewed this potent American import with alarm; a hybrid of white jazz, black blues and youthful sneer, it contrasted sharply with the dance music and romantic crooning familiar to listeners of the BBC's Light Programme, the kind of popular music strictly regulated by traditional (and interdependent) publishing, recording and broadcasting interests.

18

Rock 'n' roll music kicked at traditional escapism with unseemly arrogance and gathered as its disciples young men known as Teddy Boys, the first great post-war irreverent youth movement to be identified by their clothes, their music and their general disrespect for authority, class and established values. Right on cue there appeared a hitherto unknown species of human, the teenager, and a massive generation gap which promptly split a society founded on and governed by the principle of "elders and betters".

*Rock Around The Clock* was a rallying point and by the time Pete absorbed its dubious virtues, had been on general release for over a year. The title song, performed by Bill Haley and The Comets, had been a Number One selling record in Britain but Haley was an uncharismatic fellow and many assumed – or hoped – rock 'n' roll music was a novelty which would soon go away. But a new performer, singularly more intoxicating than Haley, had emerged from the American Southlands and Elvis Presley, in turn, inspired a host of others including some lively, if derivative, Englishmen.

Rock 'n' roll music was fast catching on. It would not go away. Pete saw *Rock Around The Clock* four times that week in Douglas.

The first guitar, that year's Christmas present from Grandma Denny, was so badly set up as to be impossible to play. Pete tried hard – "fought tooth and nail" – but cast it aside in frustration after a year, and acquired instead a banjo. With only four strings to fret over, the chording was simpler and the plinkety-plonk was an integral part of traditional jazz, the type of music that now enjoyed a transient popularity on the record charts, vying with holdovers from the ballad era, souped-up folk music called Skiffle and the new, all conquering rock 'n' roll.

Three boys from Pete's age group at Acton CGS had already formed a trad jazz group. They called themselves The Confederates and was led by another fourteen-year-old called John Alex Entwistle who played French horn with the Middlesex Youth Orchestra and the bugle with a Boys' Brigade company. John, the only Confederate to have benefitted from any formal music training – he had taken piano lessons from the age of seven – invited Pete to join.

Pete made just one appearance with The Confederates at the Congo Club attached to Acton's Congregational Church. Their repertoire, culled from the likes of Kenny Ball and Acker Bilk, included *When The Saints Go Marching In* and *Marching Through Georgia*, but interest soon faded. The quartet dispersed in childish acrimony after Pete clocked the drummer in the school playground and when sympathies went with the loser, Pete was ostracised by all. All, that is, except John Entwistle.

So Pete turned his attention back to the guitar and acquired a 'new' one from his mother's antique shop. He practised with a determination fired by the thought that girls might fall for a guy who played guitar and within weeks his fingertips hardened and the changes from A to D became fluent. "I knew bloody well that I was immature compared to a lot of other people, sort of stunted emotionally. So I felt that a couple of years in a bedroom learning the guitar wouldn't do me any harm at all. When the other kids were out dancing or listening to records, I was learning the guitar."

Cliff Townshend encouraged his son and passed on advice about scales and chords, key changes and progression. Like every other aspiring guitarist of the day, Pete took notice of The Shadows, the instrumental outfit led by guitarist Hank Marvin, a bespectacled, rather clerical-looking fellow with a solid red guitar whose crystal clear lead lines picked out the simple melodies on the many hits his group recorded. Pete learned Hank's lead lines by rote but took the trouble to follow the rhythm chords used by Bruce Welch, The Shadows' other, less prominent six-string guitarist. He felt more comfortable playing rhythm chords; rhythms were what drove a band.

"In the beginning the ones who influenced me most were people like Lonnie Donegan," Townshend has said. "Lonnie Donegan and the skiffle he and many others played were the reasons that I first picked up a guitar. That was where the popularity of the guitar in Britain first began.

"It was hard for me to relate to what was happening. I never even really liked people like Buddy Holly. The only group I liked was the Shadows. It stopped there. I didn't even like Cliff Richard. I was as interested in Acker Bilk and Ken Colyer as I was in rock 'n' roll artists. Rock 'n' roll, when I was a kid, meant the Shadows, not Eddie Cochran, not Buddy Holly, and not Chuck Berry. I never heard of Chuck Berry until I was in art school."

Pete maintained his friendship with John Entwistle and it wasn't long before they put together a second group. This quartet called themselves The Aristocrats and/or The Scorpions and concentrated on Shadows' numbers, but like The Confederates they soon disbanded. John, a fan of "twanging" American guitarist Duane Eddy, built himself a bass guitar from diversely assembled component parts and they again appeared at The Congo Club but it seemed to Pete that the atmosphere was deteriorating as members aged through their teens.

From his spot on stage he observed sexual activity, petty villainy and occasional violence, the kind of behaviour often cited as rock 'n' roll's legacy to the world. It was the closest Pete ever came to being in a gang and it might well have stirred his earliest thoughts about what he came to see as rock's most basic responsibility: its potential and power to benefit, not plague, society.

Musical aspirations at Acton County Grammar School were not confined to Pete and John and their classmates. One year ahead of them, a millenium in schoolboy terms, was a tough troublemaker called Roger Daltrey who, at fifteen, was removed from the school for a variety of misdemeanors and a reluctance to wear the school uniform. Unlike Pete or John, Roger Daltrey was a confirmed Teddy Boy with cascading quiff, turned-up collar and a correspondingly aggressive personality.

Roger was the kind of boy that parents warned their children to avoid. Raised in the back streets of Shepherds Bush as a deferential youngster, he changed overnight with the advent of rock 'n' roll. He listened to Lonnie Donegan and Elvis Presley and modelled his appearance accordingly. He was quick with his fists; what you wanted, Roger believed, had to be fought for, but all he'd so far managed to acquire was a job in a sheet metal factory and a home-made guitar which he played in a semi-professional band called The Detours.

The Detours was Roger's band and none of its changing

complement dared suggest otherwise. It was actually earning money from sporadic appearances at private functions and its members had been recruited – as was often the case – on the strength of their equipment. A Vox amp was a passport to joining, and woe betide its owner if he disputed Roger's right to use it. A smack in the mouth generally settled such disputes.

John joined The Detours first. He was approached by Roger in the street, auditioned a week later and recruited there and then. In a matter of weeks John suggested that Pete be brought into the group to replace a departing guitarist and not long after that their drummer, away on holiday at the time, was unceremoniously bumped to make way for Doug Sandom, a bricklayer seven years older than the rest of the boys. Roger himself played lead guitar while the singer, the on-stage front man, was a Danish bacon sales rep called Colin Dawson. Disagreements between Roger and Colin were regular and abrasive.

It is difficult to imagine two more different temperaments than Pete Townshend and Roger Daltrey. Pete was shy, retiring, self-conscious, nervous on stage, an introvert; Roger was outwardly flamboyant, an extrovert, tough, aggressive and loud-mouthed. Pete was tall and skinny; Roger was short and stocky. Invariably, Roger had his own way.

Poverty dictated the continued use of home-made instruments; John made bass guitars from half-inch plywood, attached his own pick-up, put on a few false knobs for effect and painted the finished product red. Roger, too, was an aspiring luthier and with the help of his father made solid electric guitars for himself and Pete, as well as impressive large speaker cabinets which cunningly concealed the embarrassing meagre speaker inside. Groups who carried around masses of large equipment scored an important psychological victory over those with tiny speaker cabinets.

The Detours' original performance schedule was haphazard, firms' outings, the occasional youth club, but Pete's mother took a keen interest in their fortunes. Occasionally she fixed up dates through her music business friends and drove the group to and from shows in an overcrowded van. Their repertoire was unashamedly predictable – cover versions of popular songs, instrumentals, even a smattering of trad jazz with Roger gamely toting a trombone – and Colin Dawson tended to assume a separate identity as a featured performer with his own backing band. This aggravated the friction between him and Roger who was the group's real driving force. Soon he was ousted to make way for other singers in a succession of brief, unsatisfactory combinations.

Shortly before Dawson left, The Detours was auditioned by a local agent called Bob Druce who ran a chain of dance halls in West London and appears to have had a virtual monopoly on pubs that presented groups as in-house entertainment. The audition was successful and The Detours found themselves working three or four nights a week, sometimes travelling as far afield as Broadstairs on Druce bookings while maintaining a lucrative sideline with private functions set up by themselves.

One day The Detours found themselves playing a support spot to Johnny Kidd and The Pirates, a group whose complement included just one guitarist, singer, bass player and drummer. It had a marked effect on both Pete and Roger.

Not long afterwards Roger abandoned his guitar and became the singer. Pete took over as sole guitarist. John turned up the volume on his home-made bass. With Sandom still performing adequately on drums, the nucleus of The Who was born.

The third generation of the Townshend family to make his career from music was off and running.

# CHAPTER TWO

Roger worked at the sheet metal plant, John had a job in a tax office and Doug stacked bricks. Pete, however, had no plans for a daytime job at all. Occasionally, he took on a delivery round for a local butcher and, on the suggestion of his dad, toyed with the idea of working for Decca, the record company, in its electronics department. Much more appealing, though, was the possibility of going to art college and at the age of sixteen he signed on for a four year course at Ealing Art School where, unbeknown to him, a minor revolution was taking place between the old guard and a group of young progressive lecturers whose ideas he came to admire profoundly.

Most would be rock musicians who went through art college in the early sixties – John Lennon, Eric Clapton, Keith Richards, Ray Davies – spent their time playing guitar when they should have been in class, or listening to imported American rock 'n' roll instead of studying homework. Few paid much attention to what they were being taught but the atmosphere at these institutions was always supportive to any kind of artistic endeavour. The students themselves provided a ready audience for their errant but musically inclined colleagues.

By and large, Pete was an exception to this trend. He never graduated in graphic design but kept his eyes and ears open. A natural seeker with a mind so open as to be positively famished for extracultural nourishment, he took in almost everything that Ealing Art School offered, both academically and socially.

Much of what he absorbed between 1960 and 1963 went through a sorting process and turned up in his music and ideas for years to come: The Who, their records and their image, became an indirect product of Ealing Art School.

Pete left Acton CGS for the Art School in the summer of 1960 and, though the college was but a short bus ride from where he lived with his parents (and two younger brothers) near Ealing Common, opted to share a flat even closer to the college with another student, writer and designer Richard Barnes. "It wasn't as if I'd had rows with my parents or anything like that," he explained later. "It was just that I wanted to do exactly as I liked – play records right through the night if I wanted to."

The atmosphere at the college, the free and easy lifestyle, was a sharp contrast to the constricting diet at grammar school and it had an instant and profound effect on the hitherto withdrawn teenager. The introvert vanished overnight. He joined CND and the Young Communists League. "There was a newness about art college, having beautiful girls around for the first time in my life," he said later. "It was such a great period... very exciting."

Pete immersed himself in everything and everybody: music, art, girls, drugs, Detours, friends, foes, heroes and villains. Like a vacuum cleaner scouring the carpet after last night's party, Pete sucked in every influence available, all the while aided and abetted by his friend Barnes. "Pete's life evolved around art school, playing four or five nights a week, getting stoned and absorbing American blues and jazz," wrote Barnes in his Who biography *Maximum R&B*. "He went to sleep to music and woke up to music, usually the slow, lazy rhythms of Jimmy Reed. Art school also gave him a self-confidence to go with his new music sophistication."

Pete and Barnes stumbled on a piece of good fortune that was another's misfortune. They had befriended an American student called Tom Wright, a comparatively worldly fellow who introduced them to marijuana and his impressive collection of imported albums, but Wright's drug habits became exposed and he was deported. Pete and Barnes inherited his flat – and the one hundred and fifty plus record collection.

A treasure trove dropped into their laps: the slow, walking blues of Jimmy Reed, the urgent staccato rhythms of Bo Diddley, the joyous celebratory music of Chuck Berry, the sensual intensity of Slim Harpo, the precise harmonies of The Everly Brothers and the choppy economy of down-to-earth Snooks Eglin. Pete became hooked on the earliest stirrings from Tamla Motown, The Impressions and The Miracles, and listened also to the modern jazz and light classical records that Wright left behind. He systematically waded through the pile, soaking up an electric and epicurian influence that would have been quite unobtainable – and unaffordable – but for the chance intervention of a zealous drug squad.

But although music and marijuana occupied much of Pete's working hours during art school days, the college curriculum was also a source of much deep fascination. After years of restricting conservatism, it had lately come under the influence of a new head tutor, Roy Ascot, whose revolutionary new ideas included a fiendishly vague art/science called cybernetics, the study of control and communications applied to animals (or humans) and machines. When applied to art – and music – this gospel offered limitless opportunities for experimentation and Pete was quick to grasp any audio-visual ideas which could be worked into a group performance.

Certain more specific influences also emerged from art school, notably the autodestructive art of Gustave Metzke, an eccentric local musician called Andy 'Thunderclap' Newman and pop art, the work of painters like Larry Rivers, Andy Warhol and Pete Blake. In 1961, Blake produced his famous painting The First Real Target, a bull's eye design which would adorn The Who's clothes in the near future.

Metzke gave a lecture at the school and, some recall, actually destroyed an ancient double bass before a group of astonished and impressionable students. When Pete started smashing guitars early in The Who's career he cited Metzke as a major influence and even invited him to a few shows. He is reported to have been impressed by what he saw.

Thunderclap Newman gave a lunchtime concert of experimental music at the Art School and impressed Pete with his oddball sense of composition, the light and shade of his extended melodies performed on the piano accompanied by kazoo and metronome. Newman was a tape-recorder boffin and when they finally met he explained to Pete the potential of tape-recorders to double-track and thus facilitate the process of composition. It was as valuable a lesson as any Pete would receive during this period.

All these diverse influences ultimately found voice in The Detours though inter-group relations, especially between Pete and Roger, were far from rosy. The urbane singer, who still worked in a sheet metal factory, was hard pressed to keep up with the intellectual ideas from the new guitarist and arguments often resulted in violence. As the eldest member and founding father Roger took it on himself to make group decisions and Pete's broadening repertoire did not sit comfortably with him.

Doug Sandom recalls Pete being particularly unpleasant at times. "He could behave like a complete bastard and often did," he recalls. "Thoroughly obnoxious for no reason at all."

Their repertoire was gaining in sophistication according to the influences that Pete embraced even though a certain tension, inter-group rivalry, was present. The group included two James Brown songs, *Please, Please, Please* and *I Don't Mind* in their repertoire, and an early version of Mose Allison's *Young Man Blues* which they would continue to perform at various times over the next ten years. Less ambitious material – Top Ten tunes – was sandwiched between the new and exciting R&B numbers but it wasn't until he heard Bob Dylan's early records that Pete considered writing his own material for the first time.

The first complete song that Pete wrote was called *It Was You*. The Detours recorded the song in a makeshift studio that belonged to a friend of Pete's father and, though it was never released, the tape went the rounds of various publishers and was eventually recorded by a undistinguished British group called The Naturals and also used as a "B" side by Mersey-siders, The Fourmost.

Towards the end of 1962, while Pete was still at Art School and The Detours had been together for almost two years, The Beatles appeared in the charts for the first time. The following

January, The Beatles topped the charts with *Please Please Me* and the 'beat boom' was off the ground.

On a general level pop music had settled into a rut since the rock 'n' roll explosion in the fifties. By an unfortunate twist of fate many of rock's early pioneers had been silenced in the years that followed: Presley was in the army, Chuck Berry was in jail, Buddy Holly and Eddie Cochran were dead, Jerry Lee Lewis disgraced and Little Richard apparently born again to Christianity. Pre-packaged pop, safe and unthreatening, re-appeared in the charts but this was only the visible, commercial, tip of a largely invisible iceberg. The lessons of the early American rockers had not been forgotten and beneath chart level thousands of British beat groups stood in the wings, honing their craft in readiness.

The Beatles opened the gates and the flood came pouring through. Those who already had a few years experience under their belts, The Detours among them, were ideally situated. They changed their name to The Who for the first time that year on the suggestion of Pete's pal, Richard Barnes, and not long afterwards acquired their first manager, a Shepherds Bush businessman called Helmut Gordon. His credentials inclined more towards the length of his pocket than the breadth of his imagination.

Gordon bought the boys some new clothes, equipment and a van and in their travels around the club and pub circuit The Detours had an opportunity to observe other groups in action, among them The Rolling Stones and Johnny Kidd and The Pirates. Both were influential in shaping Pete's approach to playing the electric guitar.

In later years, Pete acknowledged Keith Richards as the original inspiration for his arm spinning motion, though the Rolling Stones' guitarist never seems to have played in this way since the Stones' very early days together. Yet the power of the Stones impressed Pete enormously; Jagger's looks and sexuality were undeniable and in some intangible way Pete saw himself and The Who as substitutes for The Rolling Stones. This thought was to give him an idea for a song three years later.

From Mick Green, the sole guitarist in Johnny Kidd's Pirates,

Pete picked up ideas on combining lead and rhythm play; the style known as 'power chording', propulsive play punctuated by an occasional dramatic slash across the strings, suddenly dampened or allowed to ring on uninterrupted for as long as the instrument is capable of sustaining.

Thus the newly-christened Who drew on ideas from all angles. "Pete was swinging his arm while I was in the band," says Doug Sandom. "He was working on ideas with feedback too... putting an amplifier on a chair so that it was in closer line with his pick-ups. He was smoking marijuana too, which the rest of the band didn't join in with.

"I can remember a night at Eel Pie Island when we played two sets. During the interval Pete went off outside to have a smoke... he played far better during the second set."

For all his loyal service Doug Sandom was the odd man out in The Who. His drumming was steady and unobtrusive but it lacked the aggression that fuelled the three front men, and unlike the others he was not reconciled to the idea of making a full-time career from playing rock 'n' roll music. He was a decade older, married with a family, and his work on the construction sites seemed too secure to jeopardise. The final straw came after an unsuccessful audition for Philips Records, who rejected The Who because of Sandom's limitations. After a sharp exchange of opinions with Pete, Doug was out. "I haven't spoken to him since," says the mild-mannered drummer.

For a few weeks The Who played on with a succession of different drummers until one night at the Oldfield Hotel in Greenford when a slightly drunk youth, dressed from head to toe in orange, suggested that he could perform better than that night's stand-in. He auditioned on the spot by playing *Roadrunner*, damaged a borrowed drum kit and was hired immediately.

"From the time we found Keith, it was a turning point," said Pete. "He was so assertive and confident. Before that we had just been fooling around."

Keith Moon was an extraordinary find, a drummer as naturally talented as any on the West London – or any other – circuit and perhaps even more so. He brought to the group an almost manic sense of rhythm, a fearless, arrogant style of playing quite unlike anything Pete had detected in other drummers. Until his entry into The Who he'd played in another Bob Druce act called The Beachcombers, whose speciality was surf music, the kind of superfast rock 'n' roll that demanded a drummer to whom the art of rolling tom-toms was second nature. This love of surf music on Moon's part clashed with Roger's growing fondness for rhythm 'n' blues music and Pete's penchant for a hard and powerful rock sound but the intermingling of styles would become an enormous asset for The Who as a collective whole.

Keith later claimed to have deliberately engineered the circumstances of the spontaneous audition. He was just turned seventeen at the time with a carefree personality and a sense of humour that rivalled his recklessness on the drum kit. Much of his time was spent laughing or drinking.

Thus reconstituted, The Who quickly assumed a reputation as the brashest band on the West London pub circuit. A sense of urgency now permeated their show, from Keith's abandoned flurries to John's tutored indifference, from Pete's howling guitar to Roger's deep need to enforce his leadership by competing for attention.

Their next leap forward came from a source as propulsive and urgent as the band itself.

\* \* \* \*

It is the Mods' misfortune to be remembered solely as delinquent gangs who laid waste the beaches of Southend and Brighton during bank holiday weekends. In actuality the riots and subsequent publicity virtually stopped the movement in its tracks. The clashes with rockers were a sideline to the real Mod interests: soul music, clothes, dancing, pep pills, staying out all night (or all weekend) and, above all, looking cool.

The Mods developed as a reaction to the scruffiness of both beatniks (college scarf, chunky sweater and beard) and rockers (dirty jeans, leather jacket and greasy hair). The Mod movement began slowly around 1960 and grew dramatically after the media focused attention on the troubles by the sea. Before then, though, the Mods enjoyed their lifestyle free from public gaze and were to be found in various West End clubs, the forerunners to discotheques, where they danced to American soul music, always checking the mirror to keep the image razor sharp.

The best known Mod Club in London was The Scene in Ham Yard near Piccadilly Circus and among its patrons was Pete Meaden, part-time publicist for The Rolling Stones, friend of Stones' manager Andrew Oldham and a Face among the faces. By a happy coincidence Meaden patronised a barber in Shepherds Bush who also cut Helmut Gordon's hair. Jack the barber thus became the intermediary that brought Pete Meaden into contact with The Who.

At first Gordon hired Meaden as The Who's publicist. Meaden was hooked on image building and, not unnaturally, decided to turn The Who into Mods, not just sartorially but intellectually. "I had this dream of getting a group together that would be the focus, the entertainers for the Mods, a group that could be the same people onstage as the guys in the audience," he said later. "Instead of just listening to R&B records, I thought how great it would be to have an actual representation of the people. Although they were separated by the stage, they had all the necessary factors for audience identification. Townshend identified with the Mod scene immediately."

The first stage in Mod indoctrination was accomplished easily: clothes were bought with Helmut Gordon's money and their name was changed to The High Numbers, a Mod expression which indicated peer group admiration. The music they played, the soul and R&B, was tailor-made for the Mod market and the growing abandonment of their stage show was entirely in keeping with the fast and furious lifestyle to which the Mods subscribed.

"The name was perfect," said Meaden. "I dreamed of it one night. High – being a little high – and Numbers was the name for the general crowd. There was a hierarchy situation with the Mods and The High Numbers gave them a step in that hierarchy."

Meaden arranged for The High Numbers to perform at the Scene Club and took Pete under his wing. He offered them a handful of Drynamil tablets, purple hearts, which were gobbled down eagerly by all the group. Suddenly they were expanding their audience way beyond the confines of Shepherds Bush and West London.

"The Scene Club was the centre – it dictated everything," said Pete later. "From there outwards it all happened. That was where the whole thing began, where the breed, the fashion thing, the violence thing came about. And there was the Goldhawk Club which was amazing. I used to spot all the major fashion changes at the Goldhawk Club, nowhere else. You'd see one guy wearing a pair of sneakers with buckles and you'd know that the next week they'd all be wearing them. And sure enough, they all were."

Meaden was anxious to exploit the new-found popularity of The High Numbers and a deal was arranged for Fontana, a label under license to Philips Records, to release a single by the group. He selected a Slim Harpo tune called *Got Love If You Want It* which was already popular with Mods and re-wrote the lyrics to appeal even more strongly to the new audience. Retitled *I'm The Face*, it was released in June of 1964 with a similar artefact *Zoot Suit*, on the 'B' side.

It was not a success. Philips pressed up only a thousand copies and though Meaden made some earnest inquiries as to how it could be bought into the charts, the only sales seemed to be to Meaden and the group themselves, some of Pete's college friends and John's grandmother.

"To be quite blunt about it I think we exploited the Mod situation," said Pete with hindsight. "Rock music isn't a working class phenomenon; at least, it isn't in my opinion. But the Mods *were* working class – they worked. They left school at fifteen, still living with their parents, big sisters and younger brothers, and they were going through all this family turmoil while they were working at jobs; and so their leisure hours were spent with an appetite for pleasure and a bitterness for life and work that we weren't used to.

"I'd been brought up by a fairly well-to-do musician who was neither lower, middle or upper class – Dad was classless. We had working class friends and we had posh friends and I didn't work except for a few paper rounds to get guitars. I never *really* worked. I stayed on at school, picked up a couple of GCE's, went to art school fooled around. I never did anything except play with the group.

"I always felt incredibly moved by the Mod thing. It was glamorous and young and fresh, and I felt it was something with which I wanted to be associated. It was slick, it was American, it was rock 'n' roll. The Mods had an incredible taste in music compared to what it is today."

Though the single flopped, Meaden maintained his unflagging energy. Helmut Gordon was persuaded to put the group on contract and pay them a weekly wage of twenty pounds each. Roger quit the sheet metal factory, Keith gave up his job as a salesman for British Gypsum, John handed in his notice at the Income Tax office and Pete left the art school. When he told the tutor of his intentions, the tutor was astonished to learn that Pete could make twenty pounds a week playing guitar. He advised Pete to become a professional musician right away.

But the contract with Gordon was invalid (they were all still under twenty-one, then the legal age of majority) and further outside input was needed before The High Numbers could succeed on their own terms. It arrived one night in September 1964 during their weekly encounter with the Mod crowd at the Railway Hotel, Harrow. It arrived in the form of a well-dressed gentleman, so oddly out of place among the regular patrons that Richard Barnes thought he was a man from the Council, checking to see whether the tightly packed room represented a infringement of fire safety regulations.

# CHAPTER THREE

Of all the many influential characters that have crossed paths with Pete Townshend, few affected him so deeply as Kit Lambert, the eccentric impresario who co-managed The Who with Chris Stamp from late 1964 to the mid-Seventies. Lambert was a man of keen intelligence, witty, artistic and a *bon vivant*, but he was also painfully neurotic, a homosexual given to delirious excess, an alcoholic and, at times, a helpless drug addict. But he was a creative manager in every sense of the word, a genius in the art of pop promotion, and from him Pete learned sophistication and how to think big, to turn grand ideas into reality, and to camouflage grim prospects with wild infectious optimism.

Kit was born in Knightsbridge, a classy area of central London, on May 11, 1935, and raised in an atmosphere of emotional insecurity cushioned by material comforts; the son of a composer whose artistic career earned more than a measure of controversy and the product of a broken home from the age of four. He was conceived in Vienna on a night when Constant Lambert gave a piano recital to a hostile reception and the following day his mother Camile organised a protest against the unfriendly criticism.

Constant Lambert distinguished himself during the twenties by becoming the first British composer commissioned to write a ballet score for the celebrated Russian dancer Diaghilev and for sixteen years he was Music Director with the Vic Wells ballet in London. He was a generalist in the arts: In 1934 he authored

*Music Ho!*, a noted critical and reference work and he took an interest in fine art to the extent that Kit was christened after painter Christopher Wood.

But Constant Lambert was intemperate – he cited a lingering childhood illness as the reason for his drinking – and, it is widely believed, fell deeply in love with Margot Fonteyn who remained a close friend throughout his life. His stormy marriage to Camille ended just before war broke out in 1939 and Kit was raised by his mother, grandfather and an aunt and uncle at a house in Peel Street, Notting Hill Gate.

Both his parents remarried but Constant Lambert died from bronchial pneumonia in 1951 aged forty-six. Kit is said to have boasted that he wouldn't outlive his famous father and, in fact, died one month short of *his* forty-sixth birthday in 1981. A memorial service for Constant Lambert was held at St. Martins In The Fields and he is succinctly remembered in The Oxford Companion To Music as an artist whose "stature as a composer was perhaps lessened by the energy he devoted to conducting and other activities."

By this time Kit had spent five years at a private preparatory school in the coastal town of Worthing and moved on to Lancing College, a public school in Sussex. Here he specialised in modern languages, acted in school plays, and became President of the Debating Society but is remembered as being emotionally unstable, unable to cope with his parents' divorce, a reckless talent of occasional brilliance. He won an open scholarship to read language at Trinity College, Oxford, but his academic career was interrupted for two years by conscription; Second Lieutenant Lambert served with the Royal Artillery between 1954 and 1956 and, for a period, was posted to Hong Kong.

At Trinity, Kit was a profligate student, cultured, charming and generous in the extreme. His first taste of showbusiness came when he was appointed publicity manager to various dramatic productions and, convinced by the artistic strength of eye-catching visuals, opted for a creative career in the film industry. To this end he studied for six months at the Paris Film School in 1959 and landed his first job as production assistant

-- a euphemism for gopher – on a British made picture called *West Eleven* where he could observe director Michael Winner at work.

In 1961, an old school friend called Richard Mason proposed that Kit join an exploration team to Brazil to find an unknown river, the Iriri. Kit became the team's official photographer but the dangerous enterprise ended in disaster: hostile natives attacked the party with bows and arrows, Kit defended their encampment with a revolver, Richard Mason was killed in the raid. Kit buried his friend beside the Iriri while banner headlines at home proclaimed "British Explorer Murdered".

Safely back in England and thoroughly shaken up by the episode, Kit joined the BBC – where he met Chris Stamp – as a production assistant, and became fascinated at the prospect of producing a film which would portray the excitement of the mushrooming pop industry. Stamp was an unlikely partner for Kit, a dour hustler whose background was in marked contrast to his own, working-class and tough, uncultured but fiercely competitive. He was the brother of actor Terence Stamp, the son of an East End tug-boat driver, logical to a tee and, in the words of Nik Cohn, "approximately ruthless".

Lambert and Stamp left the BBC together and worked freelance on various productions at Shepperton Studios near Staines. Together with a school friend of Stamp's called Mike Shaw they searched for a pop group to star in their conceptual documentary and they had almost given up the search when, in September of 1964, Kit came across The High Numbers at The Railway Hotel in Harrow. He was attracted by the crowd outside, the crush of Mods on their Vespa scooters. The next two hours changed his life.

What he saw that night was a group quite unlike any he had already seen on the search around London's clubs. The High Numbers' stage performance did not ape The Beatles who dressed in suits, bowed low after each number and generally behaved like an experienced, if lively, cabaret act. The High Numbers' show was based purely on themselves and the needs of their audience as seen through the eyes of Pete Townshend.

The High Numbers didn't so much perform as explode. Roger

Daltrey delivered a song from way below his throat, scowled aggressively and punched the air to relieve his frustration. Occasionally he took the microphone from its stand and scraped it against Keith's cymbals or chucked it in the air, spinning on its lead like a South America bolas. Behind Roger, Keith Moon was a blurred flash of white as he skated around the drum kit, little rolls and flurries kicking the music into shape, while John Entwistle simply stood there deadpan, twanging away, bored silly.

But the centre of attention on stage was Pete. Several times in each song his arm curled around in a wide arc, slashing upwards at the strings on his guitar; his legs danced as if the floor was too hot to walk on and from time to time jumped into the air and swayed like a child's toy with a round base that never capsized. He shook his guitar and carried it close to the speaker cabinets to induce feedback which stammered out like morse code as he played with the pick-up controls and dampened strings with either hand. For all the world he appeared as a madman possessed by the loud music he was himself producing.

Pete realised full well that his talent on the guitar lay not in any ability to play it with the accuracy or even emotion of the jazz and blues players from whom most British guitarists took their cue. First and foremost he was a rhythm man, chords and bass strings to the fore, but on a secondary level he was a sonic pioneer who used the guitar purely as a *sound source*. In this role, formal technique was unimportant; the squeaks and screams, the unexpected rumble and the uninterrupted whine demanded a head for invention, not fingers for fretting. Music theory came a poor second to sound and self-expression.

And this was why Kit Lambert's eyes danced in the back of his brain the night he first saw The Who on stage. "The atmosphere in there was fantastic," he said later. "The room was black and hot. Steaming hot. And the audience seemed hypnotised by the wild music. Pete Townshend was already producing feedback from his guitar and amplifier. As soon as I saw them I felt a total conviction that this was it. It's as simple as that. This was it – Bingo!"

The attraction was by no means one-sided. By the second half of 1964 The High Numbers had grown increasingly restless under the patronage of Helmut Gordon and though Pete Meaden was a continuing source of inspiration (and good times), he was insufficiently equipped to deal with the practicalities of managing a group. Genuine advancement seemed as elusive as ever.

Lambert took his pal Chris Stamp along to a High Numbers' show in Watford later the same week and the ambitious duo promptly decided to scrap their film plans in favour of taking over The High Numbers' management. In the event, this turned out to be little more than a formality: Gordon's contract was invalid (the boys being under age) and Meaden was prepared to sell his interest in the group for five hundred pounds. Unlike Gordon, though, Meaden remained friends with them for life and, in later years, benefitted from Pete's altruistic charity.

To The High Numbers, Lambert and Stamp must have *seemed* like a bolt from the blue; influential wheeler-dealers with the necessary panache, credentials and connections to whisk them out of obscurity with a flick of their garrulous tongues. But the bottom line was considerably less promising. The new management team knew practically nothing about the record business or how to find work for groups, were absolutely ignorant – even delinquent – about financial affairs and, despite outward appearances, lacked the necessary capital to provide for the group on anything other than the shortest of short terms. Nevertheless they promised the group members one thousand pounds a year each and signed a (legal) contract which ensured them of forty percent of the band's earnings for years to come. It was an unusually large slice of the cake.

What Lambert and Stamp did have, apart from savings of around two thousand pounds, was an enthusiasm for the job that bordered on mania. The offices of New Action Ltd, the company they formed, were at 84 Eaton Place in Belgravia, but the imposing address belied the chaos that went on inside. "As solemn management it has always been farcical," wrote Nik Cohn, a journalist who was privy to the complex reality of New

Action Ltd. Other accounts substantiate the accuracy of this observation.

Aside from their enthusiasm for the job, Lambert and Stamp – especially Lambert – had a less tangible influence on the group best described as worldliness. In this respect the leading characters were Pete and Kit. Recognising Pete's potential as the group's creative force, Kit took it on himself to provide an education in the ways of the world. He taught Pete (and Keith) the art of fine living, which wines to order in the best restaurants, and he introduced Pete to yet more musical influences, baroque classics, the music his own father had enjoyed and the music of Purcell, Sir William Walton and Darius Millhouse.

Pete moved into a flat above the Belgravia offices and at Eaton Place there materialised Pete's second make-shift studio. (The first, with two mono tape recorders, had been above his parents' flat in Ealing). Lambert acquired two better tape recorders, Revox stereo models, and offered suggestions while the guitarist produced demos of his own compositions.

"Kit had a great grasp of musical terms and was able to make a critique," said Pete later. "He used to throw in a lot of ideas and make suggestions that seemed to be completely inappropriate, but whenever I tried them they used to work."

It was the beginning of a working method that is quite unique in rock. First Pete would painstakingly overdub each instrument, guitar, bass and drums, and then add his own voice on top. The finished tape was then circulated among the rest of the group who learned their respective parts in time for an actual recording session. "But these recordings lack one thing," he said later. "And that is excitement. There's no presence, no spur-of-the-moment feel about them. Everyone knows that if there's an effect there, it must have been thought out in advance."

Though Kit Lambert tried to conceal his homosexuality, Pete soon realised the truth and turned a tactful blind eye to the stream of delicate young men who came visiting and, more often than not, appeared at the breakfast table. Soon all pretense was abandoned and Kit took Pete and Keith to dine

39

in gay restaurants and even introduced them to Quentin Crisp.

Despite their inexperience, the new management team, with the help of assistant Mike Shaw, were operational in other areas of promotion. They put together a primitive lighting rig for the group to use on stage and made a short film of them (after all). This was not only shown to potential bookers but used on stage as an introductionary sequence to a High Numbers' performance. They travelled around London in search of new venues for them to play, fixed them up with a temporary job backing a girl singer called Val MacCallum (with whom they appeared at a concert in Blackpool headlined by The Beatles) and even promoted their own concerts with varying degrees of success.

Their most successful stroke was to persuade The Marquee Club, London's premier West End rock haunt, to book the group each Tuesday night for several weeks. The Marquee season – which coincided with their decision to revert back to calling themselves The Who – was an extraordinary success. Though the first night attracted only a handful of paying customers, word of mouth spread fast and within three weeks The Who had broken The Marquee's box-office record.

The group's powerful stage routine was primarily responsible but the management team did not slouch on the promotional aspects of their job. Several areas of London were flyposted – Maximum R&B was the chosen slogan – and a casual fan-club called The Hundred Faces was formed from their Mod following. Also, perhaps even more important, Pete Townshend had started to trash equipment on stage.

The first time this occurred was at the Railway Hotel, Harrow, towards the end of 1964. "I started to knock the guitar about a lot, hitting it on the amps to get banging noises and it had started to crack," Pete told his friend Richard Barnes. "It banged against the low ceiling and smashed a hole in the plaster and the guitar head actually poked through the ceiling. When I brought it out the top of the neck was left behind."

The incident provoked a smattering of laughter from the audience and Pete realised that to save face he would have to make it appear as if the gesture was deliberate. "I just got really angry and smashed what was left of the guitar to smithereens.

I just picked up another guitar and carried on playing as if I'd meant to do it."

On the next night that The Who played at The Railway, an expectant audience was disappointed until Keith smashed his drum kit. A week later Pete and Keith both trashed their equipment at the same time and from henceforth The Who's name would be indelibly linked with the smashing of equipment, though Pete was hard pressed to maintain a steady supply of guitars. "I had to almost start stealing guitars," he said. "At Jim Marshall's music store in Hanwell they had heard about me breaking guitars and thought that I wouldn't keep up the payments on a broken guitar. One day I just grabbed a Rickenbacker off the wall and ran out. Eventually they sent me hire purchase papers for it."

Soon Lambert swallowed his concern over the expense, informed the press of this revolutionary tactic and encouraged Pete to smash instruments regardless of the cost. "I would only do it when I could afford it or when there was time to get it repaired or get another instrument for the next day," he recalled. "At one time I was making payments on eight guitars."

Clearly the next step was to find a new record outlet for The Who but, despite their increasing popularity as a live attraction, record companies were unwilling to commit themselves on the strength of the demos that Pete was producing at Eaton Place. In the end it was a chance encounter with American expatriate record producer Shel Talmy that brought The Who a singularly unattractive record contract with American Decca, an offshoot of the parent Decca organisation in London.

There were several flaws in the arrangement. The Who were contracted to Talmy and not directly to the record company which meant that their royalty rate, already tiny, was further eroded by Talmy's slice of the action. Also – and ultimately even more frustrating – Talmy was entitled to be The Who's exclusive record producer for an eternity. From this shabby foothold, The Who's recording career began.

Among the songs that Pete had recorded at his make-shift studio was a number called *I Can't Explain* which was ideally suited to the Mod following. For the first recording session under the new contract at London's Pye Studios near Marble Arch Shel Talmy, unsure of Pete's ability on guitar, brought along session player Jimmy Page and The Ivy League, a trio of singers who specialised in falsetto harmonies, to sing back-up. In the event, Page was only called upon to play on the "B" side, an unmelodious blues shouter called *Bald Headed Woman* which was written by Talmy himself.

"Talmy never said a word to me," said Pete. "I said to him 'Oh no, I'm the lead guitarist in this group'. It was incredible, like a Love Affair* scene, and we were The Love Affair of 1965. We were The Who but so what? A few chart successes and then we were out. We were on something like half a per cent."

(* The Love Affair were a British group who charted three times in 1968. They were involved in a public controversy when it became known that they had not played on their records.)

*I Can't Explain* more than mitigated the deficiencies of the "B" side. The sharp riff is clearly influenced by the guitar on records made by The Kinks – also Talmy clients – but the overall sound blends echoes of The Beach Boys, rhythm 'n' blues and the seeds of a musical strain that would eventually be termed heavy metal. Equally important, the lyrics suggested deeper thought than the meaningless escapism served up as lyrics on the vast majority of singles released at this time.

In what would become a pattern for the future, Pete used Roger as a mouthpiece through which to articulate his own emotions, and in this instance Roger was cast as a frustrated Mod. The song's romantic theme is secondary to its outlet as a more general teenage reflection: too young to know, not old enough to find out. By anyone's standards it was a classy record and though Pete's name was spelt incorrectly on the label, The Who's vinyl debut brought a measure of success from which they would never retreat.

"I wrote *I Can't Explain* about a kid who couldn't explain to a girl that he loved her. A couple of months later it was on the charts and I started to look at it closely and I realised that the song was on chart not because it was a little love song but because it openly paraded a sort of weakness," recalls its author.

*Explain* was released in the third week of January 1965, and

42

reached Number Eight in the UK charts after a couple of TV appearances by the group. One, on the BBC's Top Of The Pops, was a lucky last-minute stand in appearance but the other, on Rediffusion's Ready Steady Go!, would have important repercussions during the coming year.

And so The Who were seen by a mass audience for the first time. They were an odd bunch. Unlike other televised rock groups (including The Rolling Stones at this time) they dressed differently and appeared not to communicate too closely with each other during the delivery of each song. But the jerky isolation of the individual performers was mitigated by the overall sound of the music they produced and the apparent desperation of the performance.

On his first RSG! appearance Pete wore a check shirt and hipster slacks in an identical style to that which Paul Weller of The Jam would wear twelve years later. But it was not what he wore that defied convention as the way he looked: quite the ugliest fellow to turn up in a pop group for many a day, and neither was his sallow complexion redeemed by the features of the rest of the band. In the case of the Beatles, Ringo has been aptly described as the "runt of the litter"; in the case of The Who, each member was the runt from four individual litters.

Sociologically, The Who were British rock's first genuine anarchists, punks to a man (with the possible exception of John Entwistle). With managerial encouragement, they refused to conform to accepted patterns set down by their immediate predecessors, the Beatles-inspired groups of 1964 who comprised much of what came to be known in America as the British Invasion. Their individuality stuck out like a sore thumb and Vicki Wickham, the assistant to the producer of RSG!, loved them. "Of all the groups on Ready Steady Go!, The Who most typified what the show was about," she said. "Ready Steady Go! was instant pop music. It was every trend before it happened and things came and went super fast." The Who, henceforth, became regular performers on RSG! and their second single, released in May, was chosen as the show's theme song.

"Our next single is pop-art," Pete announced to the music

43

press. "We wrote it with that intention. The lyrics are young and rebellious. It's anti-middle class, anti-boss class and anti-young marrieds."

The campaign to promote The Who as pop art in tandem with *Anyway Anyhow Anywhere* took on epic proportions as the group eased gradually away from their Mod image and sought, as The Beatles were doing, to intellectualise their appeal. The equipment trashing was not mere violence but "auto-destruction" no less and the clothes they now wore – Union Jack coats, T-shirts with vivid designs and military insignia – harked back to Pete's art school experience. "We stand for pop art clothes, pop art music and pop art behaviour," Pete told interviewers after taking instruction from Kit Lambert. "We don't change off stage. We live pop art."

*Anyway Anyhow Anywhere* was released in May and again Roger acted as a mouthpiece to communicate Pete's frustration but in this context his self-confidence was resolute. "Nothing gets in my way, not even locked doors," he sang, and to observe Pete on stage was to appreciate the sincerity, or at least the implications, of his attitude.

By this time Pete was still living above the management office in Belgravia but not often did he wake up to observe the comings and goings at the foreign embassies that populate this area of London. Chart success enabled The Who to widen their sphere of operations and for most of 1965 they performed for whoever would book them, preferring one night stands in clubs than traditional package shows, and earning an average fee of one hundred and fifty pounds against sixty percent of the door takings. But the money, although it rose gradually throughout the year, was not sufficient to finance their lifestyle, the wrecking of equipment, the clothes, the devil-may-care attitude inspired by Kit Lambert and now adopted, in various degrees, by the group themselves.

Pete spent his wakeful hours – and that meant twenty hours a day or more – saturated in the group. He was either writing, giving interviews, performing, travelling or arguing with the rest of them and the management team who in turn were arguing with Shel Talmy and Decca Records. The success of

*Can't Explain* generated a disappointing financial return and, awakened to the realities of the contract they had hastily signed, Lambert and Stamp re-negotiated for a better royalty. This source of discontent was matched by the personal relationship between the four musicians; it had never extended much further than the actual music and a noticeable rift now developed between Roger and Pete and, eventually, between Roger and the rest of the group.

"We get on badly," said Pete in an unusually candid interview with the music press. "Roger causes a lot of trouble because he is never satisfied with the sound and is the only one who will speak about it. Roger is not a very good singer at all in my opinion. He has got a good act but I think he expects a backing band more than an integrated group. I don't think he will ever understand he will never get a backing group."

"Pete's got a bit of a chip on his shoulder," retorted Roger. "Mooney and I used to get all the birds whereas he, as the writer, was the most creative and probably thought he should have all the attention."

The cabin-like atmosphere in which all the principals existed cannot have helped. Neither can Roger's realisation that the group he once lead was slipping away from his control, that his leadership had been undermined creatively by Pete and logistically by the management, and neither can the pills they were all taking, the alcohol they were drinking. Tantrums were two a penny.

"We used to physically fight on stage," admitted Roger. "I used to call Townshend a cunt and he'd call me a git and hit me with a guitar and I'd be banging him with a microphone and we'd think 'Christ that's a good sound'. We lost our tempers with each other and took it out on our instruments."

Between road trips, Pete worked on material that would appear on The Who's first album. Among the songs was a slow blues called *My Generation* which Lambert at first dismissed. So the tempo was changed, the words re-phrased to enhance the mood, the feel of the song – its rage and resentment – improved by upward key changes and a coda of reckless cacophony. It was released as a single at the height of The Who's internal conflicts and its success, both artistic and commercial, was without question the most potent argument for keeping the group together.

"The Mod was trying to justify himself," wrote Nik Cohn. "(He) wanted to lash back at everyone who'd ever put him down, but he'd taken too many pills and couldn't concentrate right. He only stammered. He was mad, frustrated, but he wasn't articulate; he couldn't say why. The harder he tried, the worse he stammered, the more he got confused. In the end he got nowhere."

The record was a stunner. It rose to Number Two in the UK charts (Number One in Melody Maker), the highest position a Who single would ever reach. It became an anthem, the group's best known brag, and like it or not, Pete would be obliged to live with its sentiments for eternity.

"It's a very big social comment," Pete said after a year's reflection. "It's the only really successful social comment I've ever made – some pilled up Mod dancing around, trying to explain to you why he's such a groovy guy, but he can't because he's so stoned he can hardly talk. People saw different aspects of the record. It was repetitive, there were lots of effective key changes in it so it didn't bore you too much, and there was a bit of feedback at the end to keep people happy. It was our biggest seller and we never hope or want to produce anything like it again."

Its release coincided with what would become the first of several internal Who spats to reach the press and place the group's future in doubt. On September 23, in Copenhagen, a furious dressing room row ended with Roger knocking Keith out and on their return to England Pete, John and Keith insisted that Roger leave The Who when outstanding commitments permitted. "He was thrown out for interfering with our lifestyle," said Pete. "Keith, John and I really liked drugs and he didn't."

Various alternatives were explored for the future. Boz Burrell, of Boz's People, was suggested as a replacement for Roger but he turned the group down and Kit Lambert unenthusiastically proposed that Pete form a new group with Paddy, Klaus and

Gibson, a trio managed by Brian Epstein. He also toyed with retaining The Who as a trio, with Pete on vocals, but in the end Lambert and Stamp persuaded the other three to re-admit Roger on the understanding that he curb his aggression. After some humming and hawing they agreed.

"Originally the group was run by the iron hand of Roger," said Pete later. "He used to be very tough in getting his own way and if he didn't he'd shout and scream and stamp and in the end he'd punch you in the mouth. Kit intervened and said why don't you give him another chance so we said to Roger... in the future if you want to make a point, it's got to be done sensibly, so no more getting things done by violence. Roger said from now on he'd be Peaceful Perce and I don't think he's raised his voice since."

In December, The Who's first album – also called *My Generation* – appeared in the shops. Recorded in seven hours flat, it has since been criticised by Pete as an uneven hotch-potch of material compounded by Shel Talmy's unsympathetic production and inter-group disagreements over which material should be included. Roger, as always, favoured cover versions of strong r&b material that were performed on stage but Pete, with management backing, felt his own compositions deserved more space. In the end a compromise, favouring Pete, was reached: eight originals and four covers.

Whatever Pete's misgivings, *My Generation* remains one of the most influential rock albums ever recorded, a blueprint for punks everywhere and a shining example of the truism that short cheap recording sessions enforce creativity in a way that lengthy studio sessions seldom do. On all the tracks the instrumental work is astonishing in its drive and power to surprise, especially when placed in context with the safe style of playing that contemporaries favoured.

On many songs Pete continues to experiment with guitar sounds, adding feedback and switching between pick-ups to produce the "electric" feel, hitherto explored only by Jeff Beck of The Yardbirds. But none of the propulsive guitar work would have been possible without Keith's drums offering a springboard for solos that other guitarists must envy to this day. The best guitar solo on the record, *The Kids Are Alright*, is launched by Keith, sustained by Keith and brought to a climax by Keith.

As has been pointed out by others, Keith's early drumming took over the parts traditionally played by a melodic lead guitar. This freedom allowed Pete to alternate, to play a loose rhythm yet tumble in with louder chords when the occasion demanded. On other occasions, when a more traditional solo technique is required, as in James Brown's *Please Please Please*, Pete's efforts are nowhere near as impressive.

If Roger's crude singing flaws the album, the underlying pitch is of a caged animal wanting out. The rumbling, moody bass, the tension and release of the drums, and the often distorted guitar are stretched to the limit.

"From my point of view that first album was just miserable," says Pete, of what has since become regarded as a classic and, incidentally, now sells for upwards of twenty pounds in its original sleeve. "There was no fun at all. The only track I liked was *The Ox*, the free-for-all instrumental. The rest was really disciplined and I thought the demos were better."

# CHAPTER FOUR

At the end of 1965 Pete Townshend was close to the centre of the young and glamorous world of British pop. His creativity was now informed not just by the immediate Who inner circle and his own personal experience but by a vast outpouring of talent that recognised no limits, a competition so fierce that no group could rest on its laurels – that would come later – or lay claim to a status greater than the reception afforded its most recent chart single.

In his new Chelsea flat Pete lived a life where the dividing line between levels of reality blurred as a vanishing rainbow. There was the public, Pete who was seen, as were all pop stars, as having won the football pools and who consequently must enjoy a life-style to match; a celebrity who knew other, greater, celebrities and had access to the highest levels of pop consciousness; a revered figure, a leader. His schoolboy brag – to "push this huge hooter at them from every newspaper in England" – had materialised.

Then there was the other end of the rainbow. The kitty was empty, debts mounting, and the six principals directly concerned with The Who's prosperity were continually at odds, either as individuals or *ad hoc* factions. A seventh, Shel Talmy, required careful handling or imminent expulsion.

There was also the reality of being only as good as your last single, of knowing that unless he came up with another good song The Who could not continue to exist on the terms they had laid down for themselves. Only sustained creativity on

Pete's part could sustain The Who.

The first business of 1966 was for Lambert and Stamp to extricate themselves from the contract with Shel Talmy. This was brought home to Stamp on a trip to America early in the year and the discovery that US Decca was principally a classical label with little or no knowledge of how to promote pop groups. There were other problems, financial and creative, and true to form the management approached the matter in cavalier fashion, took the law into its own hands and forced a showdown that could only end up across a courtroom floor.

Without any legal justification the management wrote to Talmy to the effect that his "services were no longer required" and The Who simply switched record labels. Their fourth single *Substitute* was issued on Reaction, a label formed by Robert Stigwood, the group's agent, and distributed by Polydor. Its "B" side was a song called *Instant Party* which, in actuality, was to have been their next single under the Talmy agreement. It had already been recorded with Talmy under a different title: *Circles*. Such blatant contract breaking inevitably led to court action.

"We did two versions of *Circles*, said Pete. "Both were identical because they were both copies of my demo. Shel put in a high court injunction saying there was a copyright in recording; in other words if you're a record producer and you produce a song with a group and you make a creative contribution then you own that sound.

"He took it to the High Court Judge and he said things like 'On bar thirty-six I suggested to the lead guitarist that he play a diminuendo, forget the adagio, and lay thirty-six bars modulating to the key of E flat', which was all total bullshit. He used to fall asleep at the desk and Glyn Johns, the engineer, used to do everything."

It was Pete's first experience of the law and in the end an out of court settlement was reached between Talmy and the group. Talmy was no longer the group's producer and in the UK they were free to record for Reaction; in the US they stayed with Decca and Talmy retained a percentage of The Who's record royalties for the next five years. This enabled the producer to amass a small fortune from The Who's subsequent success.

For inheriting The Who, Polydor stumped up fifty thousand pounds in advance royalties and US Decca came up with fifty thousand dollars. Kit Lambert took over as the group's producer though the new single *Substitute*, as fine a song as any that Pete has written, was recorded with the group producing themselves.

"The *Substitute* session was a bloody amazing session," recalled Pete. "Keith couldn't even remember it afterwards. That was the first Who produced session. Kit didn't slide naturally into the seat of producing The Who – he kind of arrived at the position of producing The Who because we desperately needed a producer. It was obviously logical that I should produce The Who even then. So it was logical that when it came to *Substitute* and we got out of Shel Talmy's clutches we should enjoy ourselves.

"It was an amazing time in The Who's career. We were more or less about to break up. Nobody really cared about the group. It was just a political thing. Kit and I used to go for walks in Hyde Park and talk about what was left of The Who combining with Paddy, Klaus and Gibson."

*Substitute* reached Number Five in the UK charts and, like *I Can't Explain*, was retained in The Who's stage show for perpetuity, a catalogue classic with a tremendous guitar riff and, especially on its single pressing, the kind of bass part for which John Entwistle could be justifiably proud. Unfortunately the resonance of the bass has been lost on later album collections.

Sometime during their musical discussions in the first half of 1966, Kit Lambert suggested to Pete that instead of restricting his output to three and a half minute singles he might try to compose more conceptual pieces, to create a song cycle of greater substance than a simple chart hit. It was this suggestion that led to The Who's eventual vocation as creators of extended works, and *I'm A Boy*, their second official single of 1966 (Decca continued to release old tracks throughout the year), began life as the first such project.

Pete's original idea was a rock opera called *Quads* which took as its basis the concept that in 1999 parents could pre-determine the sex of their children. In Pete's story a family had requested four girls but through a slip-up one of the children turned out to be a boy. The family raised him as a girl anyway and the song *I'm A Boy*, with a guitar part influenced by the music of Purcell, was his cry for individuality.

It was another hit, the second of three curiously conceived singles released by The Who this year. The third *Happy Jack* told the story of a dimwit who passed his time playing with children on the beach. "That was just my memories of some of the wierdos who lived on the sand," Pete explained later. "There was no character called Happy Jack but I played on the beach a lot on the Isle Of Man when I was a kid."

But the most extreme example of Pete's preoccupation with out-of-the-ordinary subject matter and extended composition came on *A Quick One*, The Who's second album, released after many delays in December. Its centre-piece was the title track, a nine minute-long mini-opera in which several short songs were linked together with instrumental passages to tell a vague story of marital infidelity. It was a crude beginning to the kind of music that would later surface on *Tommy*.

*A Quick One* was a five part song in which the central character awaits the return of her husband from a year long journey. Her vigil is interrupted by the arrival of a lustful fellow called Ivor The Engine Driver (sung in a comical deep voice by John Entwistle) who takes advantage of her lonely circumstances in unexplained, but indiscreet, ways. After a mock country & western interval the husband returns to forgive his wife for whatever took place which brings the tale to a happy conclusion. It is in the final song *You Are Forgiven* that the seeds of *Tommy* can be found in both the counterpoint vocals between Pete and Roger and in the chord sequence that underpins a rather grandiose finale.

"It was Kit who conceived the idea of an extended pop work," Pete admitted later. "He suggested that we write an opera to fill in a ten minute gap on an album called *While He's Away* (later retitled *A Quick One*). No-one writes a ten minute song... how can you sustain interest? I just linked up about six pieces

52

of music and it was very successful".

*A Quick One* was released in December to great anticipation. In order to raise extra cash for the boys in the band it was suggested by the group's publisher that if each member of the group could contribute at least two tracks to the album, they would each be entitled to a five hundred pound advance in royalties. John had no trouble coming up with his quota and neither, of course, did Pete. For Roger and Keith the task proved a deal more onerous: Roger managed just one song but Keith, in the end, managed to satisfy the publisher with a surreal instrumental called *Cobwebs And Strange*, the nearest thing to a drum solo that The Who would ever record. The session, according to Pete, was as surreal as the finished product.

"It was written as a whistle and completed as a circus act," he said. "We all marched around the studio playing it. John was the only one really playing anything... he had a trumpet, Keith had a tuba, Roger a trombone and I believe I had a bass drum. And that was just the backing track."

Though far from an unqualified commercial success, *A Quick One* raised the ante considerably as far as The Who's peers were concerned. Paul McCartney was moved to declare that The Who were the best up-and-coming group in London and for the first time The Who found themselves not only rubbing shoulders with, but being compared to the upper bracket of British rock. Pete's confidence soared.

"Just after we'd finished *A Quick One* we became a big clubbing band," said Pete. "We used to go down the clubs a lot and I got to know McCartney pretty well. He was really raving over the album and saying that the track *A Quick One* was exactly the sort of thing The Beatles were working towards. He said they'd really been inspired by it. And when *Sergeant Pepper* came out I remember very smugly thinking, 'It's all because of *A Quick One*'.

The album came hot on the heels of The Who's first and only original EP *Ready Steady Who!*, five tracks already premiered on the Ready Steady Go! TV show earlier in the year. Though the title inferred that it was a live recording, the EP was actually a studio recording of two of Pete's songs, *Disguises* and *Circles*, and three non-originals. Two of these *Barbara Ann* and *Bucket T* represented a musical detour along surfing lines, doubtless suggested by Keith Moon, while the third, *Heatwave*, harked back to the days of Mod audiences in the Scene Club.

It had been a prolific year for Pete and his opportunities for writing had been sandwiched between live appearances up and down the country and on the Continent. On occasions The Who still performed two shows in one night, sometimes at two different venues, and the problem of constantly enduring eachother's company never really went away. In May there was a flare-up at Windsor's Ricky Tick Club when John and Keith arrived late and Pete took out his frustration by "accidently hitting Keith on the head with my guitar". Ten days later, after Keith had apparently left the group in disgust and been persuaded by Pete to rejoin – "There's no other drummer I want to play with" – Pete was involved in a car crash on the MI while returning from a show in Morecambe. This led to erroneous reports that Roger had been killed in a traffic accident, rumours that Kit Lambert fanned with all the enthusiasm of his natural PR instincts.

One important show before a large audience was at the Windsor Blues Festival – a forerunner of today's Reading Festival – on August 30. Unsure of the crowd's response, Pete unleashed his destructive zeal as never before: guitars were smashed, speakers ripped apart, drums hurled across stage and Roger kicked in a row of floodlights while Keith hurled buckets of water into the audience. From the edge of the stage Lambert and Stamp threw smoke bombs into the melee and watched in suppressed delight as the crowd, inspired by Pete, smashed several rows of seating. To their minds, the publicity was compensation for a damages bill that reached into four figures.

By the end of the year, after a final appearance on Ready, Steady, Go! and a show with The Pink Floyd at London's Roundhouse, Pete and The Who could reflect on having realised their ambitions in England and, more crucial in the long term, finally settled many of the personal differences that had almost wrecked their prospects twelve months earlier.

54

Though Pete and Roger would never quite see eye to eye, Pete told Melody Maker's Nick Jones: "There are four soloists in this group. On our own we'd fly off at tangents but now we've rehearsed carefully and we all sing in harmony and unison and there is a kind of orderly disorder."

Whatever satisfaction regular chart success brought was still tempered by the shaky financial situation. Record royalties of ten percent of the retail price were immediately halved by Shel Talmy's settlement and the remaining five percent was further eroded by a forty percent cut towards management. Earnings were continually being eaten up by the excesses of the stage show but Pete had become bored with smashing guitars and the destructive climax was dropped for an important showcase appearance at London's Savile Theatre with Jimi Hendrix on January 29.

A friendship had developed between Brian Epstein, the new owner of The Savile, and Kit Lambert and this pairing was a pointer to the aesthetic changes that pop was undergoing as the sixties came of age. A dividing line was being drawn between pop and rock; groups were no longer expected to please both the older, more sophisticated, listeners and screaming girls at the same time. But with artists like Hendrix at one end of the spectrum and a slew of pretty-faced pop idols at the other, The Who found themselves adrift somewhere in between.

Early attempts to promote The Who had been aimed at the teenybopper market (interviews with Fab 208, discussions on where they bought clothes, the "D" notice of Roger and Keith's marriages) but the group, and Pete especially, were a long way removed from the fresh-faced cute look that teenyboppers demanded of their idols. In this respect The Who paid a price for being performance pioneers. Whilst the here-today-gone-tomorrow teen idols had merely to shake a leg and smile to inspire crowd hysteria, The Who had gone all out to offer a visual spectacle. Now, with the tide turning, they were between two stools: because of their aggressive stance the teenyboppers were scared.

Another factor that inhibited their progress was that unlike

The Beatles or The Rolling Stones – the only two established British acts to rival their potential – The Who had yet to make any impression in the USA, the biggest market place of all. Their only exposure across the Atlantic to date was a smattering of pre-taped sequences broadcast on the Shindig TV show but none of these had taken their records far up the US chart. *I Can't Explain* had been a local hit in the Detroit area where a cult of Who fans had mushroomed through the support of a radio station but *My Generation* managed only ninety-seventh position in the Billboard Hot 100. It was reported that American Decca, perplexed by the feedback climax, hesitated to release this record, thinking the noise was a fault on the master tape.

Clearly the only way out of The Who's financial problems lay in American success and, though they had delayed longer than their rivals, the American campaign was scheduled to begin in March. Chris Stamp, taking over the responsibility for the US while Lambert concentrated on Europe, arranged a series of shows in New York City in March 1967, and a curious but attentive audience, primed by reports from England, sat back in anticipation.

To describe The Who's American debut as explosive would be an understatement. All thoughts of dropping the destruction from their act – as they had now done at home – were dismissed and for the first show at the RKO Theatre the group, and Pete in particular, turned the stage into a veritable Hiroshima. Compere/promoter Murray The K, the disc jockey who claimed to be the "Fifth Beatle", was visibly shaken by the sight and the audience reacted with disbelief.

For five days The Who performed five shows a day and on each occasion they played just three songs: *I Can't Explain*, *Substitute* and *My Generation*. Since *A Quick One* had yet to be released in America, US Decca re-promoted their first album, now called *The Who Sings My Generation*, and word began to spread. As had been the case in England, The Who had to be *seen* to be fully appreciated and this series of concerts attracted a clique of fanatically dedicated fans who would remain loyal for eternity.

By the end of the week The Who destroyed five guitars,

twenty-two microphones, four speaker cabinets and a sixteen-piece drum kit. Their most recent US single *Happy Jack* reached Number Twenty-four on the Billboard Hot 100 but the trip was still a financial disaster. Aside from the equipment, which was glued back together by roadie Bob Pridden or replaced by Chris Stamp after hastily arranged endorsement deals, the group's hotel bill was swelled by reckless living. The Who's reputation as immoderate hotel guests was launched on this trip.

The brief American debut was followed by a trip to Germany and The Who returned to the UK in time for the release of a new single, *Pictures Of Lily*. "It's all about wanking," admitted John Entwistle in his usual down-to-earth fashion. "It's Townshend going through his sexual traumas. I sometimes think you could say that that record represents our smutty period or, to be more refined, our Blue Period."

"It's all about a boy who can't sleep at night so his dad gives him some dirty pictures to look at," said Pete. "Then he falls in love with the girl in the pictures which is too bad because she's dead."

The song had been inspired by an old vaudeville star called Lily Bayliss whose picture Pete had spotted on the wall of his girlfriend's flat. Inevitably there was a degree of controversy surrounding the record – which Lambert and Stamp, as always, did their best to stir up – but that didn't stop it reaching Number Four in the British charts.

*Pictures Of Lily* was the first Who record to appear on Track Records, a new label set up by Lambert and Stamp as a means of raising extra cash. In the coming months, Track would expand considerably and attract such artists as Jimi Hendrix, Arthur Brown, Marsha Hunt and a group called John's Children whose principal writer was guitarist/singer Marc Bolan. As the business of Track took up more and more of their time, Lambert and Stamp delegated the day-to-day management of The Who to a recently appointed production manager, John Wolff.

By this time, Pete had moved into a large studio flat on the top floor of a building in Soho at the corner of Wardour Street and Brewer Street, just around the corner from Track's offices in Old Compton Street. Like his previous residences it doubled as a recording studio, resembled a hi-fi showroom even, while the actual living accommodation was cramped and unwelcoming. He had taken to spending free evenings at the UFO Club in Tottenham Court Road, a gathering place for the revolutionary new left where all-nighters were held in a psychedelic atmosphere provided by the music of the Pink Floyd and a liquid light show beamed on to the walls and ceilings.

The UFO Club was an important underground centre in the mid-sixties, a place where ideas were exchanged between counter culture icons of all persuasions. Established originally as a means of raising funds to support The International Times, it soon developed into a place to score acid and hashish, to socialise, to pull girls and to discuss the politics of revolution. Pete had already experimented with acid and at the UFO he had access to high quality LSD from the Swiss Sandoz laboratories; like the rest of the UFO's hip clientele he could spend an evening gently tripping the night away, his eyes locked into the bubbles on the wall, his mind somewhere else entirely.

Among the other regulars at the UFO Club was a stunningly attractive girl called Karen Astley, a clothes designer and illustrator whose comely face adorned the Night Tripper poster on the club's walls. Like Pete, Karen had been to Ealing Art School and her family background was steeped in music; her father, Edwin Astley, was a well known composer and classical arranger. Pete became enamoured with Karen, she became his first (and only) serious girlfriend and soon they would set up home together at a flat in Ebury Street near Sloane Square in Belgravia. They were married a year later.

Karen joined the entourage for The Who's second US trip of 1967. Their most important engagement was at the Monterey Pop Festival over the weekend of June 18, a huge gathering of receptive hippies and a showcase for many important new acts both English and American. It was an ideal opportunity for The Who to present their music to exactly the right kind of audience they were seeking in America and, apart from some equipment problems and a sharp exchange between Pete and Jimi Hendrix over whether Jimi was copying Pete's act by destroying guitars, The Who's performance was a splendid success.

The assembled hippies – fifty thousand or more – were astonished by the aggression of The Who's show; they exploded in an orgy of destruction, the like of which could scarcely have been imagined amid the love and peace rhetoric that descended on San Francisco that summer.

Backstage at Monterey Pete met Stanley Owlsley, the inventor of the powerful hallucinogen STP, and on their flight home to England he and Karen sampled a concoction that Owlsey had given them. Pete was quite unaware of the strength of STP – he wouldn't have tried it if he was – and the effect was a nightmare, a far cry from the mild twenty-five minute trips he'd experienced in London with Sandoz 25.

"It was like a hundred years on the airplane across the Atlantic," he said. "I felt that if I had cut off my own head the horrible feeling would go on for an eternity because I wasn't in my body. I never realised what a fragile mind I had. Eventually it tailed off and then you get like, instead of a night's lovely planning out, nice colourful images, you get about a week of it and then you need a week to repiece your ego, remember who you are and what you are."

The experience was sufficient for Pete to make a firm decision to abandon psychedelic drugs (which the rest of The Who had never embraced with much enthusiasm anyway). He continued to smoke copious quantities of pot because he felt unable to enjoy music without it.

The Who returned to England at the height of what appeared to be an establishment campaign to incarcerate The Rolling Stones for drug offences. Both Mick Jagger and Keith Richards had received controversial jail terms and, though the sentences would soon be set aside on appeal, Pete promptly displayed a sense of solidarity within the London pop hierarchy and persuaded the group (less John Entwistle who was on his honeymoon) to record two Stones' songs, *The Last Time* and *Under My Thumb*, and release a single within days. An accompanying advertisement campaign implied that The Who would continue to record Stones' songs "to keep their work before the public" but this effort, which scraped up to Number Fourteen in the UK charts, was their only stab at the Stones' catalogue.

The third US visit of 1967 took place during August, a month of dates supporting Herman's Hermits. Unimaginable as this combination might seem today, the tour made logistical sense in 1967 simply because Herman's boys would outdraw The Who and they shared the same US Agency, Premier Talent. Nevertheless, there were mixed feelings in The Who camp since Herman fans, youthful and predominantly female, found few aesthetic attractions in a beanpole guitarist with an outsized nose and his equally unappealing cohorts. Irritated by the unsympathetic audience, Pete smashed guitars with chilling precision, barely concealing his hostility as night after night instrument and amplifier came apart in his hands. Chris Stamp, in charge of the tour, was hard pressed to maintain a steady supply of new equipment.

The Herman's tour was notable for two further incidents: Keith Moon's 'twenty-first' birthday party (it was actually his twentieth) for which The Who suffered a lifetime ban from the Holiday Inn chain, and a crash landing at one stop after their chartered plane's engines cut out. This inspired at least two romantic songs, Glow Girl and I Can't Reach You; the former's coda resurfaced in Tommy and the latter was included on The Who's 1968 album The Who Sell Out.

The Who returned to England in mid-September with the intention of spending at least three weeks in the studio working on a new album. As it was, they only managed to complete I Can See For Miles, a song Pete had written some time ago and which was originally recorded in Los Angeles earlier in the year. It was a match for anything The Who had ever done, a supremely exciting song, packed with tension, a threatening guitar drone and the kind of drumming that placed Keith Moon on a pedestal only he could have toppled.

Pete knew it was a great single and his confidence took a severe battering when it failed to become a major hit.

"That was a real heartbreaker for me," he said. "It was a number we'd been saving, thinking that if The Who ever got into trouble this one would pull us out. On the day I saw it go down (the charts) I spat on the British record buyer. To me this was the ultimate Who record and yet it didn't sell."

In the UK *I Can See For Miles* reached Number Ten on the singles chart but in America, where The Who had been concentrating their profile, it reached Number Nine, their highest US chart placing to date.

The group returned to America in November for yet another tour, this time to support Eric Burdon and The Animals. It was on this trip that they appeared on The Smothers Brothers TV show, a two song performance (*My Generation* and *I Can See For Miles*) which climaxed with a gigantic explosion. In the interests of excess Keith had loaded his drums with considerably more flash powder than necessary and the ensuing eruption singed Pete's hair and damaged his ears. He couldn't hear properly for a week afterwards, an ominous augury for the hearing problems that Pete would suffer in the coming decade.

November saw the long delayed release of their third album *The Who Sell Out*, the group's first shot at a conceptual record where the songs all follow a central theme. In this instance the theme was advertising and pirate radio and, though the concept wasn't sustained throughout, the results indicated that The Who's sound had been heavily influenced by Pete's fondness for choral music. Many of the songs rely on soaring harmonies, a direction hitherto unexplored amid the hard rock that dominated their earlier work.

At one point Chris Stamp had proposed selling advertising space on the record but there were no takers. As it was, Stamp unwittingly provided Pete with his inspiration for the concept.

"I went into Chris's office one day and found him looking at a piece of paper. I said to him 'What's that?', said Pete.

"Oh, just a list of songs that I thought might make up the next album," replied Stamp.

"Album? What album?" said Pete.

"Well, you've got to have an album out."

"But *that* and *that* and *that*," said Pete. "You're joking. What a boring old album."

In the heat of the moment, Pete launched into a stream of

consciousness idea that summed up the concept in one stroke. "I've thought of a great idea, forget all that," he said. "It's like a radio show. We all do commercials. On the cover we have the group involved in glamorous ads."

And so it came to be. "I wrote out a list of stuff that I thought would be good and John and Keith thought some up as well. And then Kit found these old Radio London jingles and put it together as a radio show. I'd conceived it as being in a radio show format, but more of a spoof on advertising than on radio, which is what it came out to be."

The album's cover featured four spoof ads with Keith modelling a giant tube of acne cream, John as a Charles Atlas strongman, Roger in a tub of baked beans and Pete with an enormous deodorant stick. Like so many other aspects of The Who's image, it caused a deal of controversy, especially as the outer sleeve contained no information relating to song titles.

Inside that sleeve was the closest The Who ever came to making a pop album. Sandwiched between the advertising and pirate radio jingles are songs with a far lighter touch than anything they had recorded before. On *Rael*, *Sunrise* (virtually a solo track by Pete), *Armenia City In The Sky* (written by Pete's friend and chauffeur Speedy Keen) and *Our Love Was*, The Who introduced an airy, ethereal quality, especially on the vocals, where Roger was gaining in confidence throughout. *Rael*, like *A Quick One*, was a collage of tunes and its instrumental backdrop, a chord sequence of disarming simplicity yet Wagnerian grandeur, would go on to form one of the major themes in *Tommy* and, later, became a dramatic *tour de force* in The Who's stage act.

Pete's writing had grown more sophisticated since he had by now mastered playing piano. *Tattoo*, with its shimmering arpeggios, and *Mary Ann With The Shaky Hand*, with its fat acoustic rhythm, came only just short of the standard set by *I Can See For Miles*. This was chosen to close side one, prefaced by a John Entwistle commercial for guitar strings: "Hold your group together with Rotosound Strings!"

Whatever it may have been, something was holding the group together firmly at last.

1968 was a strange year for The Who and Pete Townshend. With a firm foothold in the US at last, their status on either side of the Atlantic differed considerably. In England matters reached a low ebb: hit singles were thin on the ground and box-office takings dropped alarmingly as a result. From commanding fees of three hundred pounds a night upwards, The Who found themselves playing for as little as sixty pounds. They were neither underground nor pop and all but a hard core of fans ignored them as virtual has-beens, holdovers from a Mod era that was now just a memory.

In America, however, they were at the forefront of the British underground simply because their music was adventurous and their stage shows exhilarating. Much of their income now came from American album sales but it was still necessary to continue touring to maintain a steady financial turnover. They were still in debt – quite how much had never been calculated nor will it ever be, since accounting was not a strong point at New Action Ltd – yet they refused to limit their spending by curbing the destruction on stage (especially in the USA) or even toning down their offstage life-style.

In this respect Pete and Keith were the chief culprits while Roger and John looked on askance. Already Roger took to watching the expenses and did not hide his concern over Keith's excesses in hotel rooms, much of which was encouraged by Pete. Roger had once been a sheet metal worker and, if The Who collapsed in a welter of debts, it seemed to him that a similarly demeaning job was his only alternative. Pete, on the other hand, knew nothing of manual work and, now an established songwriter and the only member of The Who with what might be called an independent power base, he could anticipate a musical future regardless of The Who's own career prospects. It would be unfair to imply that Roger was interested solely in feathering his own nest; he was merely being practical, assessing reality as a man whose feet were firmly on the ground. For all Pete's wayward genius, reality was not one of his strong points. Thus the tensions within the group continued despite their increasingly professional (and cohesive) outlook.

Two crucial events occurred within Pete's life during 1968. He began work on what would eventually become *Tommy* and he was introduced to an Indian spiritual figure called Meher Baba. Since the creation of *Tommy* was a gradual process, extending over twelve months, it is the impact of his guru that had a more immediate effect.

College friend Mike McInnerney, an artist and fellow habitué of the UFO Club, brought Baba into Pete's life. He had noticed during conversations that Pete's rambling philosophies coincided with spiritual ideas put out by Baba. Already a follower himself, McInnerney gave Pete a book on Baba's teachings. Within weeks Pete, ever a seeker, was hooked.

Meher Baba was born in the Indian town of Poona in 1894 and in his nineteenth year was kissed on the forehead by Hazrat Babajan, a local spiritual teacher and Perfect Master to whom he had become attracted whilst at college. A long period of intense contemplation followed and subsequent events – periods of study, divine realisation, the assembly of disciples – led to a considerable religious influence. In 1925 Baba took a vow of silence, initially to last a year, which he maintained until his death in 1969.

In the meantime Baba gathered many followers – or "lovers" as they are called – in all walks of life in the Western world as well as the East. He made few demands on them; merely to respect his values in matters of love and compassion, but he was adamantly against the use of drugs, a dictum that proved a constant battle with Pete until the eighties. (There seems to have been a kind of divine inevitability about Pete's introduction to Baba: not long afterwards Baba, who never met Townshend, was shown a photograph of The Who. Without prompting, he placed a finger tip on Pete's nose.)

Unlike the much publicised attraction between The Beatles and Maharishi Yogi, Pete's devotion to Baba went unreported, and a serious and lasting transformation occurred. He gave up smoking dope – which necessitated listening to records "straight" for the first time in years – and, according to friends, became a far nicer person to be around. He adorned his new Twickenham home with pictures of Baba, a rotund, smiling man with a handlebar moustache whose most famous exhortation, written on a tablet, was "Don't Worry. Be Happy."

In two years time Pete would write an article for Rolling Stone magazine about his feelings towards Baba. "A lot of people equate finding a spiritual master with discovering the escape clause in life," he said. "Actually it's just the opposite. All that happens is that for the first time in your life you acknowledge the fact that you've got problems instead of futilely trying to solve them. The problems become more acute but somehow less painful. Still, they don't get solved automatically. The only way in this lifetime that you can move something from A to B is to get up and fucking move it. There's no magic. What makes following Baba different to following anybody else is that you don't change at all."

Unlike other Indian gurus, Meher Baba did not require his followers to drape themselves in white robes, shave their heads or adopt any other outward mannerisms that might set them apart from Western society. So Pete kept his guru to himself and Karen (they were married on May 21, 1968, at Didcot Registry office); quite what the rest of The Who felt about this conversion has never been fully disclosed but it seems doubtful that such realistic characters as Daltrey and Entwistle or a comical madman like Keith Moon would sympathise with spiritual awakening.

Meher Baba changed Pete Townshend's life and Pete's conversion changed The Who.

# CHAPTER FIVE

I rarely leave any good ideas unused," Pete wrote in the notes accompanying The Who's 1974 out-takes album *Odds And Sods*. *Tommy* was a sackful of good ideas, some old, some new, some spiritual, some incomprehensible. Throughout 1968, on tour and at home, in hotel rooms, dressing rooms and even airplane cabins, Pete laboured on the creation of his grand design. For all concerned it was a last ditch do or die project which could either rescue The Who from insolvency and ensure their future or sink the boat with all hands.

Despite Pete's preoccupation, the show had to go on if only to maintain income. The year began with The Who's first and only visit to Australia and New Zealand, a disastrous package tour with The Faces, Manfred Mann and John Walker of The Walker Brothers. Antipodean conservatism reigned unchecked in the unsympathetic press coverage and at the end of a ten day visit Pete vowed never to return. To this day he has kept to his word.

In February, The Who returned to America for a nine week tour of ballrooms and colleges and at shows in New York and San Francisco recordings were made for a proposed live album. In Los Angeles the group recorded two songs (*Little Billy* and *Do You Want Kids, Kids*) for the American Cancer Society but both were considered unsuitable for the ACS's anti-smoking campaign. More curiously they recorded a recruitment advert for the American Air Force, a contradiction of ideals which Pete has since disowned.

That the live recording never materialised is a crying shame. The Who were at the peak of their pre-*Tommy* form as a live band, playing a set that included *I Can't Explain, Substitute, Pictures Of Lily, Happy Jack, Boris The Spider, Little Billy, A Quick One, Relax*; three Eddie Cochran numbers, *Summertime Blues, Come On Everybody* and *My Way*; *Shakin' All Over* and, as the inevitable closer, *My Generation*. In the end the process of sifting through miles of live tape proved too onerous for Pete on top of his other commitments.

As far as current releases were concerned the barrel was dry and The Who, and their record labels, were desperate for material to release. In June, Track released *Dogs*, a comical Townshend single written about the workingman's fondness for beer and greyhound racing. It was a long way removed from The Who's true 1968 perspective and, not surprisingly, flopped ignominiously. Their recording career had reached its lowest ebb.

Kit Lambert spoke of plans to issue an album called *Who's For Tennis* but, like the live set, it never materialised. It was Kit, more than anyone in the entourage, who collaborated with Pete on his ideas for a major rock opera. "It really is the most incredible thing that after two years of brainwashing himself into being a producer of top ten singles for radio play, Kit actually turned his brain inside out and came up with the rock opera... good thinking for a group who had stopped getting hits," said Pete.

"I felt strongly that I was being tied down too much to single records. I felt that if I had to say everything on a record in three minutes flat then I wasn't ever going to say very much. I wanted to find a way to stretch it a bit more without making it pretentious or pompous and without making it sound like classical music."

Pete set himself two conditions in the writing process. Firstly, the songs could be taken as a series of potential singles, listenable individually yet telling a story when strung together; secondly, they could be performed in sequence live in a way that other conceptual productions, records like *Sergeant Pepper*, could not.

The first public hint of Pete's ambitious plan came in an interview with Chris Welch of Melody Maker in May. Pete spoke of "working on an opera, which I did once before, and calling it The Amazing Journey. I've completed some of it," he added, "and I'd like to put it out on an LP. The theme is about a deaf, dumb and blind boy who has dreams and sees himself as a ruler of the cosmos."

Pete was rapidly earning a reputation as an adept interviewee. He was loquatious in a way that few rock performers ever were and he thought deeply about the nature of his art and rock's responsibility as a medium of communication. Unlike others in his profession, Pete never viewed a journalist as a potential foe; he was even inclined to use an interview situation as a means of testing the water for ideas or organising those ideas in his own mind.

Nowhere was this trait more apparent than on the night of August 15th when, after the final concert on The Who's second US tour of 1968, he spoke in San Francisco with Rolling Stone owner and editor Jann Wenner. The published interview became famous, not just because it outlined ideas for *Tommy* in detail, but because Pete was seen by the American underground to display an unusual sincerity about his work.

"The album concept in general is complex," Pete told Wenner. "We've been talking about doing an opera, we've been talking about doing live albums, we've been talking about a whole lot of things and what has basically happened is that we've condensed all these ideas, all this energy and all these gimmicks, and whatever we've decided on for future albums, into one great juicy package. The package is, I hope, going to be called 'Deaf, Dumb And Blind Boy'. It's a story about a kid that's born deaf, dumb and blind and what happens to him throughout his life. The deaf, dumb and blind boy is played by The Who, the musical entity. He's represented musically, represented by a theme which we play, which starts off the opera itself, and then there's a song describing the deaf, dumb and blind boy. But what it's really about is the fact that because the boy is deaf, dumb and blind, he's seeing things basically as vibrations which we translate into music. That's really what we want to do: create this feeling that when you listen to the music you can actually become aware of the boy, and aware of what he is all about, because we are creating him as we play."

Pete went on to describe the plot in more detail. "The boy sees things musically and in dreams and nothing has got any weight at all. He is touched from the outside, he feels his mother's touch and he feels his father's touch, but he just interprets them as music. His father gets pretty upset that his kid is deaf, dumb and blind. He wants a kid that will play football and God knows what.

"One night he comes in and he's drunk, and he sits over the kid's bed and he looks at him and he starts to talk to him, and the kid just smiles up, and his father is trying to get through to him, telling him about how the other dads have a kid that can play football and all this kind of crap and he starts to say, 'Can you hear me?'. The kid, of course, can't hear him. He's grooving in this musical thing, this incredible musical thing; he'll be out of his mind. Then there's his father outside, outside of his body, and this song is going to be written by John. I hope John will write this song about the father who is real uptight now.

"The kid won't respond, he just smiles. The father starts to hit him, and at this moment the whole thing becomes incredibly realistic. On the one side you have this dreamy music of the boy wasting through his nothing life. And on the other you have the reality of the father outside, uptight, but now you've got blows, you've got communication. The father is hitting the kid; musically then I want the thing to break out, hand it over to Keith.

"The kid doesn't catch the violence. He just knows that some sensation is happening. He doesn't feel the pain, he doesn't associate it with anything. He just accepts it."

After outlining various incidents in the boy's life, Pete described how he is ultimately able to hear, speak and see after all. "It is a difficult jump," he said. "It's going to be extremely difficult but we want to try to do it musically. At this point the theme, which has been the boy, starts to change. You start to realise that he is coming to the point where he is going to get over the top, he's going to get over his hang-ups.

"The music has got to explain what happens, that the boy elevates and finds something which is incredible. To us, it's nothing to be able to see and hear and speak, but to him it's absolutely incredible and overwhelming; this is what we want to do musically. Lyrically, it's quite easy to do it; in fact, I've written it out several times. It makes great poetry but so much depends on the music, so much. I'm hoping that we can do it. The lyrics are going to be okay, but every pitfall of what we're trying to say lies in the music, lies in the way we play the music, the way we interpret, the way the things are going during the opera.

"The main characters are going to be the boy and his musical things; he's got a mother and a father and an uncle. There's a doctor involved who tries to do some psychiatric treatment on the kid which is only partly successful. The first two big events are when he hears his mother calling him and hears the word 'Tommy', and he devotes a whole part of his life to this one word. The second important event is when he sees himself in a mirror, suddenly seeing himself for the first time: he takes an immediate back step, bases his whole life around his whole image. The whole thing then becomes incredibly introverted. The music and lyrics become introverted, and he starts to talk about himself, starts to talk about his beauty – not knowing, of course, that what he saw was him but still regarding it as something which belonged to him, and of course it did all the time anyway."

This description of what *Tommy* would eventually be about was published almost ten months before the release of the album and long before The Who went into the studio to record. It was widely read and may have limited Townshend's options as far as changing the plot was concerned, but the course was irredeemably set.

Recording sessions began as soon as The Who returned to England. Out of necessity they were crammed in between concert performances – never the best way to work – and most of October and November were spent on the road. Traditionally, The Who had released albums around Christmas time

70

but *Tommy* was far from complete by then.

In England, Track released *Direct Hits*, an album of (mostly) singles recorded since the break with Shel Talmy. In America, however, the need for instant product was more acute as regular touring over there had created considerable demand for an album. Decca botched the job miserably. *Magic Bus – The Who On Tour* was compiled from inferior masters of irrelevant material, John Entwistle "B" sides and tracks already available on earlier albums. Its title implied that it was a live recording – which it wasn't – and group and management were justifiably angry when they realised, too late, what their US record outlet had done.

Progress in the studio was slow. No title had been fixed on by the year's end though several suggestions – Amazing Journey, Deaf, Dumb and Blind Boy, Brian Opera and Journey Into Space – had been vetoed. Eventually *Tommy* was chosen because of its Englishness and association with soldiers in the World War I.

"Pete used to come in some days with just half a demo," said Roger. "We used to talk for hours literally. We probably did as much talking as we did recording. We spent weeks sorting out arrangements for the music."

"Pete had been working on *Tommy* for at least two years," added Moon with his usual sense of exaggeration. "He was writing songs and putting them together just like a jigsaw but when we went into the studio it was still in bits and pieces. Pete would say 'Well, what do you think of this bit?' and then John or someone would come up with an idea and then gradually it became a group effort."

"All I knew is that when we were recording the damn thing, nobody knew what it was all about or how it would end," muttered John. "It was only when it was decided to make *Tommy* into a double album instead of a single that it became much easier to work out the story line."

Whatever the confusion in the minds of his three colleagues and perhaps even in his own mind, Pete and Kit Lambert struggled on at the less than perfect IBC studio which had been chosen for reasons of economy. Pete was grateful to the other three for giving him the freedom to dictate the group's direction though there were times when they came to doubt his sanity. "I mean, what other three musicians would have put up with my bullshit in order to get this album out?," he pondered. "It's my apple. It's my whole Baba trip. And they just sat there, let it come out, and then leapt upon it and gave it an extra boot. It's an incredible group to write for because you know it's going to work out right."

The *Tommy* sessions dragged on through Christmas and the New Year. In December, The Who took time off to appear with some distinction in The Rolling Stones' Rock And Roll Circus, a film that has never been shown publicly, and in January, despite his preoccupation with the opera, Pete branched out with his first production work outside The Who.

Thunderclap Newman was a group assembled by Pete around the wayward talents of Andy Newman, the musician and tape-recorder fanatic he'd encountered at art school. Newman was an ex-Post Office engineer and a jazz pianist who idolised Bix Beiderbecke, and Pete put him in the studio with Jimmy McCulloch, a sixteen-year-old Scottish guitarist, and John "Speedy" Keen, the singing drummer who wrote *Armenia City In The Sky* for The Who's *Sell Out* LP and had lately been working as Pete's chaffeur. With Pete as producer and bass player (he worked under the pseudonym of Bijou Drains) the quartet recorded a Keen song called *Something In The Air*, a memorable single that would top the British charts later in the year.

Their album *Hollywood Dream* was equally impressive, indisputable evidence that Pete had mastered the art of record-making and getting the most out of a studio. The success of the single caught the group unawares and attempts to capitalise on the hit by touring met with disaster. On the road they were augmented by Jim Avery (bass) and Jimmy McCullough's brother Jack (drums) but they were an ill-assorted bunch and twelve months later they disbanded in disarray.

This unexpected success was but a minor triumph during a year of extraordinary progress for The Who. March saw the release of *Pinball Wizard*, the first taster from *Tommy* and an immediate hit despite DJ Tony Blackburn labelling the record as "sick" on Radio One. The album followed in May, rush released after long delays simply because an American tour had been booked during the summer.

*Tommy* is a milestone in rock music, a milestone in the career of The Who and a milestone in Pete's development as a composer. Despite its faults – muddy production, misleading story line, some flawed songs – the double LP incorporates intriguing ideas and musical devices that Pete had been experimenting with for most of his professional career. The strongest musical themes, of which there were several, were established immediately during *Overture* – as they would have been of a real opera – and expanded over four sides so that even on a single hearing the melodies and riffs are easily assimulated. Whatever confusion is thrown up by the lyrics, the music – a textbook lesson in rock construction – carries the whole.

Pete gave hundreds of interviews around the time *Tommy* was released and even he appeared confused about the reality of the narrative. "I think the greatest thing I've seen about *Tommy* is the Radio Times feature in which there were three interviews: one with Nik Cohn who says he thinks *Tommy* was sparked off by his book in which there is a deaf and blind pinball champion; Mick McInnerney said he thought *Tommy* came about because I was interested in this spiritual master Meher Baba; and Roger said it was Kit Lambert's idea. The point is I really don't know."

On the surface *Tommy*'s plot follows no logical pattern. A child is born deaf, dumb and blind. He is so inert that several unpleasant experiences – sadistic and drug-orientated – do not move him. Eventually a doctor is brought in to no avail but he develops a remarkable facility for playing pinball machines. An encounter with a mirror somehow provides a cure. He is worshipped as a rock star might be worshipped. He is profoundly grateful to his disciples for the inspiration they give him.

Taken literally, the plot is so slight as to be futile but set against the powerful music, *Tommy* transcends such enigmas. The strongest songs exist as potential singles outside of the conceptual framework: *Pinball Wizard*, with the most exhilarating guitar part that The Who have ever recorded; *Amazing Journey*, delicate, yet driving; *Christmas*, on which Roger outdistances even his own improving standards; *Acid Queen*, a malevolent piece for the wickedest witch; *I'm Free*, a truly great riff; and the closing song, *We're Not Gonna Take It*, with its hymnlike coda *See Me Feel Me*. The three instrumental pieces, *Overture*, *Underture* and *Sparks* are all models of dynamics, ensemble pieces where Keith Moon, given the freedom to lead, re-establishes himself as the most perfectly equipped drummer in the whole of rock.

*Tommy* was a magnificent package too. Wrapped in a triple fold-out sleeve designed by McInnerney and containing a lavishly illustrated libretto, it arrived at exactly the right moment to capitalise on the times. Its spiritual references, its suggestion of opaque psychedelia, its aloof pretentiousness (which Pete admitted) appealed directly to the ageing rock audience. It was a grand design; everything about it was designed to turn The Who into a legend, which is exactly what it did.

The group soon realised that *Tommy*'s greatest strength lay in its live presentation. "We did one day's rehearsal, did the whole thing from start to finish and that was when we realised we had something cohesive and playable," said Pete. "Keith and I went to a pub on the way back and sat there, both incredulous at how quickly it had come together. Roger had become something else and we discussed what would happen and how it would change everything. We knew we had something that was magic and that magic wasn't as clear on the album as it would have been in live performance."

*Tommy* was previewed before the London press at Ronnie Scott's Club on May 2. It was a deafening experience for all who attended, an hour's non-stop music at full tilt volume in a small room normally filled by modest-sounding jazz combos. *Tommy* was hailed as a masterpiece by critics whose ears rang for several days afterwards.

The appearance of the group had changed considerably since their post-Mod days. Roger had grown his hair and permed the golden tresses that framed his craggy face and flowed down past his shoulders. He had taken to wearing bare-chested fringed suede outfits that exhibited his tanned athletic body to maximum advantage. Keith was a white tornado behind the biggest drum kit ever assembled while John, more often than not in black, remained stationary as always. Pete now wore a white boiler suit, baggy in the leg to hide knee pads, and Dr Martin's work boots. He grew a thin beard and became almost handsome though Roger would always overshadow him in this department. Just as Roger brought *Tommy* to life with his stage presence, so *Tommy* brought Roger into the heirarchy of great rock vocalists. He shone on stage as he had never shone before, and for the first time in The Who's history it seemed as though Pete and Roger were in perfect harmony at last.

The American tour opened on May 9 with two shows in Detroit. A week later they began a two day (four show) run at the Fillmore East in New York where the opening show was interrupted when fire broke out in an adjoining building. Midway through The Who's set a plain clothed policeman jumped on stage to advise people to leave but Pete and Roger, unaware of his identity, booted him into the pit with some force. The incident led to Pete being charged with assault and fined seventy-five dollars the following week. "We mistook the policeman for some kind of heckler," he said. "We very much regret the whole thing."

It was two weeks later in Chicago that Pete realised just how powerful the stage presentation of *Tommy* had become. "Halfway through the gig, all of a sudden, everybody realised that something was working," he said later. "I don't quite know what it was but everybody all at the same time just stood up and stayed standing up. From that moment on they would stand up at the same point. It was the first time we'd created a theatrical device that worked every time."

The touring continued throughout June as the album ascended the US charts as no previous Who album had ever done. So strong was the new material that Pete abandoned smashing his guitars on American stages as he had continued to do long after breaking the habit in England. Occasionally, when the mood took him, a Gibson SG bit the dust for old times sake, as if to emphasise that these four really were the same four who toured America with Herman's Hermits two years earlier.

In many respects *Tommy* overshadowed the group. The audiences flocked to *Tommy* in a manner that an older audience might flock to *Swan Lake*. "There are people out there who think the group is called 'Tommy' and the album is called 'The Who'," Pete observed wryly. The touring was extended; the group became exhausted. They returned to England for a handful of shows during July, then returned to America to play at the Woodstock Festival, a show subseqently described by Roger as "the worst gig we've ever done."

The decision to play Woodstock had been made by Pete under duress. Kit Lambert and Chris Stamp had little interest in the logistics of touring a professional group, and administrative duties on the road had been handed over to John Wolff who consulted with Pete over when and where to accept bookings. After much intimidation, Pete agreed to perform at the Woodstock Festival on its final day, Sunday August 17.

"We waited in a field of mud for fourteen hours sitting on some boards doing nothing and doing nothing is the most exhausting thing in the world," said Roger.

"From a human point of view it was great," said Pete. "Three people died and two people were born and half a million people managed to get on together. But musically it was awful." Pete had brought Karen and their newly-born daughter Emma to New York and he was anxious to play and return to them in New York as soon as possible. The delays infuriated him, especially as backstage drinks had been spiked with acid and all the group were tripping unwillingly for several hours. To add to their troubles John Wolff was having difficulty collecting The Who's fee from the promoters.

"I got into a terrible state and rejected everyone," said Pete. "I was telling really nice people like Ritchie Havens to fuck off and things like that."

When The Who finally arrived on stage Pete kicked a photographer (who turned out to be movie director Michael Wadleigh who was filming the event) and, midway through

*Pinball Wizard*, did the same again to yippie politico Abbie Hoffman who unwisely chose that moment to make a speech of liberation through Pete's microphone. Pete whacked the acid-crazed orator with his guitar and Hoffman was last seen rushing through the crowd yelling obscenities at the stage. Pete later said that assaulting Hoffman was "the most political thing I ever did".

"*Tommy* wasn't getting to anyone," said Pete later. "By this time I was just about awake, we were just listening to the music when all of a sudden, bang! The fucking sun comes up. It was just incredible. We didn't deserve it in a way. We put out such bad vibes but as we finished it was daytime."

The Woodstock performance, regardless of how it compared to other shows on the first *Tommy* tour, put the final seal on the Who's superstar status in America. Back in England, *Tommy* was performed in its entirety at the Isle Of Wight Festival on August 30. Pete's friend Richard Barnes describes this performance as "the most exhilarating pop experience I've ever been exposed to."

After a break in September The Who toured America again, then returned home for a UK tour. In January of 1970 they undertook the most ambitious *Tommy* tour of all, a trip around Europe's opera houses that took in the Theatre De Champs Elysée in Paris, Copenhagen's Royal Theatre, the State opera houses in Cologne, Hamburg and West Berlin and the Concertgabouw in Amsterdam. In London they were turned down at the Covent Garden but accepted by The Coliseum, and in New York, later in the year, they gave two performances at the Metropolitan Opera House where Leonard Bernstein sang Pete's praises.

The Met shows gained some notoriety when Pete reacted strongly to the demands for an encore after the second show. "Fuck off," he said, clearly exhausted.

# CHAPTER SIX

The *Tommy* album clocked up worldwide sales of over a million by the end of 1969 and by mid-1970, The Who's outlook on life had changed completely. Soon they and their managers would become millionaires, their once colossal debts no more than a dim memory. Their future was assured, subsequent albums would find a secure market and concerts would almost always be oversubscribed regardless of size. They could record anything they liked, either together or individually, and, if they wanted, make a film. Red carpets were produced on their infrequent visits to record company offices, limousines transferred them from place to place. Like a handful of other rock performers, they had achieved legendary status.

Satisfying as this must have been, Pete was embarrassed by his sudden wealth. As the group's principal songwriter, his income exceeded that of the other three quite considerably but he did not spend money profligately like so many of his fortunate peers. He was at heart a socialist and such matters as tax avoidance, long term investment planning, capital asset building and stock portfolios held neither interest nor attraction. Instead of securing his financial future he spent money on establishing a Meher Baba Centre in Richmond and financed trips to India by other Baba lovers. He contributed generously to various charities; he continued to live in the same Thameside home in Twickenham, stocked his private studio with state-of-the-art equipment, bought a Mercedes Benz car and provided generously for his family without undue ostentation.

He kept around him the same friends from earlier days, cronies from art school, fellow Baba lovers, a few musicians and artists. The four members of the Who had never mixed socially to any great degree and the acquisition of wealth actually distanced them even further. Roger bought a mansion on the Sussex/Kent border, John stayed in Acton and Keith bought a pleasuredome in Chertsey. Pete tried desperately to remain down-to-earth in circumstances notorious for launching giant egos; over dinner with Karen in a moderately priced Soho restaurant he was as happy to discuss the problem of getting a suitable baby-sitter as he was to hold forth on his artistic and musical philosophy. Above all, he stayed in touch; the remote lives led by other rock millionaires were an abhorrence to Pete Townshend.

Yet underneath, Pete was quaking in his Doc Martins at the prospect of following *Tommy*. While Roger, John and Keith were content to be professional rock entertainers, perhaps the finest rock entertainers of their era, Pete was not. He looked on rock as a challenge; each achievement must be bettered; to coast was anathema to his very soul.

"Townshend is intelligent, creative, highly complex and much given to mystic ponderings, but the things that he values most in rock are its basic explosions, its noise and flash and image," wrote Nik Cohn. "So he writes stuff like *Tommy*, sophisticated as it is, and he can see that it's good, but at the same time he feels that it's a cop-out from all the things that rock lives off, almost a betrayal. And he goes on stage and smashes his guitar – simple, mindless release. But then he gets his breath back and he knows that's not it either, to deny his own brain. And so it goes on, round and round with no end."

"Townshend spent the bulk of the seventies establishing rules only he saw, leaping over hurdles he had set up himself, desperately trying to top himself over and over again," wrote Dave Marsh. "Each success was meaningless because it only created more anxiety over what came next. He went from writing about identity crisis to acting it out."

On February 14, 1970, The Who performed at Leeds University and recorded the show. Many of their recent US shows had also been recorded but Pete felt unable to wade through the miles of tape they had accumulated. The album *Live At Leeds*, released the following May, temporarily put off the problem of succeeding *Tommy*. Another proposed delaying tactic was the recording of a multi-track single with four new songs Pete had written (*Water*, *I Don't Even Know Myself*, *Now I'm A Farmer* and *Naked Eye*) and one song (*Postcard*) by John Entwistle. The tracks were recorded at Pete's own studio but the record never materialised. Most of the songs were featured on stage between 1970 and 1971 and all eventually turned up as "B" sides or tracks on the 1974 out-takes album *Odds And Sods*. Of them all, *Naked Eye*, an anti-drug tirade, was the most impressive and was retained in concert for several years.

*Live At Leeds* was specifically designed to prick the pomposity of *Tommy* and display instead The Who's original tough edge, a side of the band that had become submerged amid the grandiloquence of the opera. Many newer fans could be excused for assuming The Who to be art rock dillitantes but *Live At Leeds* put matters back into perspective. It was gut-wrenching hard rock from start to finish, a timely reminder that The Who were first and foremost rockers at heart. The playing is outstanding and included in the package was a plethora of reproduced documents from The Who's early days – date lists, contracts, posters, receipts, even writs – all papers which emphasised the group's pre-*Tommy* historical reference. The group's preoccupation with their own history, from Shepherds Bush Modism to pop art and beyond, was to occupy their creative endeavours throughout the seventies.

A single was released in February but *The Seeker* was an almost embarrassing failure after *Tommy*'s critical and commercial success. Its lyrics were deeply personal to Pete and seemed to sum up his personal dilemma: not just how to follow *Tommy* but how to exist as a millionaire rock superstar yet stay true to rhetorical ideals already stated and reinforced by the spiritual teaching of Meher Baba.

One way for Pete to appease the dilemma was to produce sideline music as a tribute to his guru and in the same month that *The Seeker* was released a curious artefact called *Happy*

*Birthday* was pressed into vinyl. *Happy Birthday*, issued on Baba's birthday, was a limited edition (2,500 copies) album of Baba tributes that included two new songs by Pete, his solo version of *The Seeker*, a version of Cole Porter's *Begin The Beguine* (one of Baba's favourite Western songs) and assorted contributions by other Baba lovers including Ronnie Lane of The Faces. The record came with a booklet of drawings, poems and essays relating to Baba.

The two new songs (*Day Of Silence* and *The Love Man*) were directly concerned with Baba. "I wrote *Day Of Silence* on July 10, which is the day that followers of Baba choose to spend without speaking, they communicate by using pencil and paper," wrote Pete in a preface to the music score. "I wrote the lyrics the day after so I wouldn't break my silence." (In 1971 The Who played Dunstable Civic Hall on July 10 – a clear case of silence breaking!)

Another outlet for Pete's potpourri of talents was creative writing. He wrote about his love of Meher Baba for Rolling Stone magazine and in the summer of 1970 agreed to write a monthly column for Melody Maker, then the most widely read and influential pop paper in the UK. The column ran once a month and occupied the best part of a whole page for nine months from August 1970 to April of the following year and its content was a far cry from the shallow and often meaningless hyperbole served up by press agents who in the past had ghost written similar columns. (A similar experiment by Melody Maker with Rod Stewart following in Pete's footsteps was nowhere near as successful; Stewart managed only three columns and the intellectual gap was wide enough to bridge an ocean).

Pete wrote about difficult and controversial matters, provoked the readers and, inevitably, confused them. He attacked the Musicians Union (for failing to provide for rock musicians), the BBC (for its conservatism) and even, to a degree, the fans of The Who (for expecting too much). He praised the extinct pirate radio stations and dwelt on a pet topic, the responsibilities that rock fans ought to feel towards their music and themselves.

Meanwhile The Who continued to tour. A six week US stay

following the New York Met appearances visited sports arenas for the first time. The Who were now too popular to perform in the ballrooms and theatres where their reputation had been wrought, and the sense of closeness they had inspired between themselves and their fans was gradually dissipated. They made a second Isle Of Wight Festival appearance in August, toured the UK during October and finished the year's work with a show in more intimate surroundings at London's Roundhouse. At this concert they were supported by an up-and-coming pianist/songwriter called Elton John and before The Who launched into *Tommy*, Pete dedicated the evening's opera performance to the bespectacled newcomer. Earlier in the year it had been announced that the Met shows would be the final performances of *Tommy*, but this was not to be. *Tommy* was gradually edited down in concert but its two best songs, *Pinball Wizard* and the *See Me Feel Me* coda to *We're Not Gonna Take It*, became permanent ingredients of the live shows.

Somehow and somewhere in the midst of all this activity, Pete stumbled on the concept which he hoped would overshadow *Tommy*. This was Lifehouse, the most extraordinary project Pete ever conceived and, with hindsight, the most impractical, far-sighted, imaginative, disastrous, incomprehensible and disorientating idea of his and The Who's career.

"The basis of Lifehouse is a combination of fiction and a projection within that fiction of a possible reality," he explained to puzzled listeners. "In other words, it was a fiction which was fantasy, parts of which I very much hoped would come true. The fiction part of it was a story I wrote called Lifehouse about a theatre and a group and about music and about experiments and about the day a concert emerges that is so incredible that the whole audience disappears."

Lifehouse was also to be a film – reportedly backed by a million dollars from Universal Pictures – which would be produced by Kit Lambert and Chris Stamp. Its original title was *Bobby*, the name of a central character, the hero of Pete's futuristic fantasy.

"It takes place in about twenty years when everyone has been boarded up inside their houses and put in special garments called experience suits," Pete told The New York Times. "The government of the day feeds them programmes through the suits to keep them entertained.

"Then Bobby comes along. He's an electronics wizard and takes over a disused rock theatre, renames it the Lifehouse, and sets it up as an alternative to the government programmes. Next he chooses a basic audience of about three hundred people and prepares a chart for each of them, based on astrology and their personalities and other data; and from their charts he arrives at a sound for each of them – a single note or a series or a cycle or something electronic – anything that best expresses each individual.

"On the Lifehouse stage there is a rock group, which will be The Who, to comment on the sounds and celebrate them. But they aren't the heroes and neither is Bobby. The real centre is the equipment itself, the amps, the tapes and the synthesisers, all the machines, because they transmit the sounds."

The Young Vic Theatre near Waterloo Station was chosen as the site for the Lifehouse experiments. Great quantities of electronic equipment were moved into the theatre and Pete presented the band with demo tapes of over thirty new songs appropriate to the project. Glyn Johns, who had engineered many of The Who's early records and was now celebrated as a producer, was invited into the project as engineer and associate producer. Pete gave many interviews about Lifehouse and even devoted one of his Melody Maker columns to the subject.

"The aim is change," wrote Pete. "A change of life-style for the band, a change of focus for the audience and a change in the balance of power that rock wields. The Young Vic becomes the Lifehouse, The Who become musicians, the audience becomes part of the fantasy. We have invented the fantasy in our minds (*well, perhaps Pete had, but the rest were not so sure*), the ideal, and now we want to make it happen for real. We want to hear the music we have dreamed about, see the harmony we have experimented temporarily in rock become permanent, and feel the things we are doing change the face of rock.

"There is a story connected with each person that will walk into the Lifehouse, but for now we have made one up for them, until we know the real one. We have music that will stimulate them to stay with us through lengthy marathon concerts and perhaps even boring filming. We have sounds that will push us a lot further than we have ever gone before, but what the results will be is still unknown."

No one ever knew what the results would be. Despite Pete's lofty aims the project came crashing down around him after a few sessions at the Young Vic. No one understood what Pete was trying to do and the more he tried to explain, the more confused and irritated he became; the others involved thought Pete was off balance. But what really crushed Townshend was the reaction of the specially invited audience.

That audience should have been directly involved with the show, responsible for inspiring the music even. It was clearly too much for a random selection of skinheads who, despite being told that the event was experimental, expected The Who to perform as they always had. "It wasn't an act, it was an evolving process – a new kind of music. But they wouldn't buy it," admitted Pete.

"Basically the project centred around The Who living with their audience," said a bemused John Entwistle. "We did a couple of experimental things down at the Young Vic but then the whole thing fell through. They wanted us to play *My Generation* and smash guitars."

It was a catastrophe of sweeping proportions for both Pete and the group. "I've worked myself on something you'll never see to the point of nervous breakdown," he said. "We've worked probably harder in the last year than ever before. I've never come across something like this before – I've always felt an abundance of energy; particularly if it's one of my projects; I've always thought I've got to push it through, put more energy into it than other people.

"In this particular case it went on and on and after about six months with no product, only problems, and only me involved in it and the rest of the group getting bored, John getting involved in making his own album, Roger ringing me up every day trying to dissuade me from doing the project, saying that what we really needed to do was go out on the road, we eventually gave up and to put it frankly we just went back into the old mould."

Disillusioned to the point of mental collapse, shattered by the realisation that he was not infallible (a realisation that Roger, Keith and John also perceived), Pete retreated to the recording studio. "I picked out a few numbers I'd had for the film project – *Pure And Easy, Baba O'Riley, Getting In Tune, Won't Get Fooled Again* and *Behind Blue Eyes*. We did a very straight album."

*Who's Next*, the record that eventually surfaced, was an absolute triumph, generally regarded as the group's most positive musical statement ever and an overwhelming critical choice as the best rock record of 1971. A trial run with Glyn Johns as producer using the Stones' Mobile studio parked outside Mick Jagger's home Stargroves produced *Won't Get Fooled Again* and, ecstatic at the results, the group took Johns' advice and recorded another eighteen tracks at Olympic Studios in Barnes. This was enough for a double album but Johns whittled the songs down to a single LP. Some of the remaining songs turned up on *Odds And Sods* or as singles.

The sessions were the most productive and creative of The Who's career. In all, the following songs were recorded: *Baba O'Riley, Bargain, Love Ain't For Keeping, My Wife* (the only John Entwistle track of the bunch), *Song Is Over, Getting In Tune, Going Mobile, Behind Blue Eyes, Put The Money Down, Too Much Of Anything, Let's See Action, Join Together, Relay, Pure And Easy* and *Won't Get Fooled Again*. The only other Lifehouse song to have seen the light of day is *Mary*, a demo of which appeared on Pete's 1983 *Scoop* LP of out-takes. The quality of these songs was a tribute to Pete's commitment to Lifehouse.

Nine of the tracks appear on *Who's Next* and the most regrettable omission is *Pure And Easy*, a key Lifehouse song and a ballad of exquisite beauty. (Its importance to Pete can be gauged by its inclusion on his forthcoming solo album and the fact that the opening lines are incorporated into the conclusion of another *Who's Next* song, *Song Is Over*).

But the crucial element of The Who's music on *Who's Next* was the use of synthesiser loops. It was the first time that this much abused new electronic toy had been fully integrated into the

85

sound of a rock band, not simply used to add effects and frills. Pete's synthesiser tapes set the tempo for many of the songs and provide a layered backdrop that liberates the musicians from previously determined roles. Glyn Johns gave The Who a clarity of sound they had never achieved before, a crispness of tone and sharpness in definition that Kit Lambert, for all his creative suggestions, had never been able to supply.

A spiralling synthesiser pattern opens the album's first track *Baba O'Riley*, setting the mood for all that follows. "This was a number I wrote whilst doing these experiments with tapes on the synthesiser," said Pete, who titled the song after composer Terry Riley. "Among my plans for the concerts at the Young Vic was to take a person out of the audience and feed information – height, weight, astrological details, beliefs and behaviour – about that person into the synthesiser. The synthesiser would then select notes from the pattern of that person. It would be like translating a person into music. On this particular track I programmed details about the life of Meher Baba and that provides the backing for the number."

The synthesiser was hypnotic and built into a whirlwind effect while Roger pitched high and mighty vocals about the "teenage wasteland" of Pete's Lifehouse dream. Of all the performances on *Who's Next*, it is Roger's that actually impresses the most. His singing had reached a new peak, typified by his melodic reading on *Behind Blue Eyes*, one of Pete's most beautiful ballads, and the full blooded scream that erupts after the second synthesiser bridge on *Won't Get Fooled Again*.

The latter is a raging political anthem. "It's really a bit of a weird song," said Pete. "The first verse sounds like a revolution song and the second sounds like somebody getting tired of it. Basically it's in the same vein as *We're Not Gonna Take It*. It's an angry anti-establishment song. It's anti people who are negative. A song against the revolution because the revolution is only a revolution and a revolution is not going to change anything at all in the long run, and a lot of people are going to get hurt.

"When I wrote *We're Not Gonna Take It* it was really 'we're not gonna take fascism.' I wrote *Won't Get Fooled Again* at a time when I was getting barraged by people at the Eel Pie Island commune. They live opposite me. There was like a love affair going on between me and them. They dug me because I was like a figurehead... in a group... and I dug then because I could see what was going on. At one point there was an amazing scene where the commune was really working, but then the acid started flowing and I got on the end of some psychotic conversations. And I just thought 'Oh fuck it... I call it the Glastonbury Syndrome.'"

The album offered many other delights: *Going Mobile*, a Lifehouse song inspired by Pete's love of motorised holidays, used a synthesiser device called an envelope follower which hooked up to Pete's guitar and sounded strangely like someone playing under water; *My Wife* was John Entwistle's best Who song to date, a beefy monster which gained even greater authority on stage; *Bargain* was a rock prayer to Baba; and *Song Is Over*, with its lilting melody, reinforced Roger's, by now, complete mastery of emotive vocalising.

Though Lifehouse itself was a catastrophe, Pete and The Who had produced the tightest music of their undulating career.

An edited version of *Won't Get Fooled Again* was released as a single in June, 1971, and the *Who's Next* album followed a month later. Both were met with unanimous critical acclaim; both made their respective charts on either side of the Atlantic. August was spent touring America and on September 18 The Who performed their biggest ever London concert at the Oval Cricket Ground in Kennington. Throughout October they toured the UK, climaxing with three nights at the newly-opened Rainbow Theatre, and in November and December they were back in America packing out sports arenas, as popular as any rock attraction in the world.

In order to reproduce the music of *Who's Next* on stage, the band performed with pre-recorded synthesiser tapes during *Baba O'Riley* and *Won't Get Fooled Again*. The new set also included *Behind Blue Eyes* and John's *My Wife* from the new LP, a twenty-minute medley of songs from *Tommy* and a backward glance towards *I Can't Explain*, *Substitute* and, as a show closer, *My Generation*. Occasionally they played *Magic Bus* and a wildly percussive arrangement of Marvin Gaye's *Baby Don't You Do It*, and two unreleased songs, the beautifully cascading *Pure And Easy* and intrinsically spiritual *Naked Eye*, were also fitted in. It was a long show. The Who gave value for money and, unlike others in their status bracket, they rarely played a succession of obligatory encores. A Who encore was a rarity and when it came it often lasted another twenty minutes.

Travelling vast distances across the American continent was now accomplished in unashamed luxury. An army of sound and lighting men accompanied the group; managers, tour managers, press agents, accountants, lawyers, record company executives, press photographers and writers swelled the party. Peter Rudge, a sharp Cambridge graduate lately employed by Lambert and Stamp, was in charge of the operation and the operation ran like clockwork, a tribute to the professionalism so much admired by Roger Daltrey yet privately despised by Pete.

The playing was in the same mould, tight and direct, and much money was invested in PA equipment which delivered a sound as loud and crisp as any group in the world. All The Who's characteristic gestures were still there: Pete's leaps and arm rolls, Roger's microphone twirling, John's vacant stare and Keith's manic energy. As a unit the group played together superbly, perhaps better than at any time in their career. Offstage they mixed only occasionally. Pete withdrew to his hotel suite to write, read or muse on his avatar; Roger found a girl; Keith went crazy; and John stayed sane. Pete expressed the view that The Who was now a "very sophisticated circus act" and when his conscience was pricked at the sight of huge box office takings he smashed a guitar and sometimes even two.

At the end of the year a compilation of early hits was assembled onto one LP and issued under the title of *Meaty Beaty Big And Bouncy*. Since many of these tracks had been virtually unobtainable in America the album was a huge success. Its release had been made possible because Shel Talmy's rights to their early material had now expired and, finally, The Who were receiving a just royalty for their work.

A single, *Let's See Action*, was released at the same time but like most of The Who's singles during this period it fell on deaf ears, reaching only as high as Number Sixteen in the UK charts. Much as Pete tried, he was unable to write singles of the same calibre as those that graced the charts during the sixties and the group's fans, sprawling cult that they were, preferred to spend their cash on albums. A second Lifehouse left-over *Join Together* was released in the summer of 1972 and this too was only a minor hit.

For The Who as a unit, 1972 was a lost year. The only concerts they performed, during August and September, were in Continental Europe and the only album product to materialise was a second solo set from John and Pete's first solo excursion, the Meher Baba inspired *Who Came First*. Roger kept a low profile down on the farm in Kent and fretted over the group's business affairs and Keith kept a high profile in nightclubs and fretted over his disintegrating marriage.

In the early part of the year Pete travelled to India to visit Baba's tomb. "When I visited Baba's tomb I felt like a speck of dust," he said. "Suddenly everything was in proportion. It only lasted three seconds yet I yearn to reach that state of excitement and pure peace again. There is a ritual there, when all his followers stand around the tomb and sing *Begin The Beguine*. It totally zapped me out when I was there. I stood up after this ritual and was crying and everything."

Pete's mystical beliefs were respected if not shared by the remainder of the group. "It's very weird to be in a group like The Who and feel that you're at a totally different stage of spiritual evolution from the others, and yet at the same stage of physical evolution," he opined. "We're all very similar as physical bodies, we enjoy the same degree of self punishment, the same music, we enjoy playing together and so on, but we have different basic ethics of how to live our lives and they don't cross.

"Deeply written into Who philosophy is the fact that each member thinks the other guy's way is total bullshit but it's all right by me. I may be putting words in people's mouths but that's probably true. So let's say I'm tolerated in my mystical beliefs although I should imagine there's a bit of fear in the group that I might grow my hair down my back and start putting out solo albums about... do a George Harrison basically.

"Previous to being involved with Baba I tended to weigh things up very carefully whereas now I'm much more impulsive; I just sort of chase my Karma around with the feeling that Baba's got his thumb on my head, so everything's all right. At the same time I haven't changed all that much. I've still got a bad temper and I'm fairly aggressive as a musician. Quite simply, I write more honestly now. I'm not afraid to write what I'm thinking despite the fact that is a case like *The Seeker* it made quite an embarrassing record."

The second of Pete's private Baba albums *I Am* was issued during 1972. It contained less direct Townshend music than the first (a lengthy instrumental of *Baba O'Riley* and a Baba prayer called *Parvardigar* which had been set to music by Pete) but the problem of these records being bootlegged had become so acute that MCA Records demanded a more business-like approach. This demand led to Pete's first solo LP, *Who Came First*.

"The company was most understanding," he said. "They merely encouraged me to put the album out through normal channels. They wanted twenty-five thousand copies of the album to distribute and offered me a dollar an album to give to Baba, a very generous royalty. I decided that if I was going to do it on this scale, I might as well do a completely fresh album."

Pete tidied up a sample of material from the two existing Baba albums, wrote a couple of new songs and added material by Ronnie Lane and other Baba lovers. The result was the first time that his by now celebrated demos had been heard in public and it gave a fascinating insight into Pete's creative process. Included on the final record were versions of *Pure And Easy* and *Let's See Action*, the *Parvardigar* prayer, the new songs *Time Is Passing* and *Sheraton Gibson*, a version of Jim Reeve's *There's A Heartache Following Me* and three other songs, one of which *Evolution*, was sung by Ronnie Lane.

Pete's nigh nasal voice dominated the record and though the Baba prayers were heavy going to all but the most deeply committed, the record was considerably more successful than John's solo LPs, an indication that Pete was the only member of The Who who could anticipate a career independent of the group.

Two other projects occupied Pete's time during 1972. The first was an orchestral recording of *Tommy* produced by American impresario Lou Reizner and the second was Eric Clapton's long-awaited comeback concert after a lengthy period of drug-induced isolation.

Pete Townshend never does things by halves, as his re-recording of the tapes that made up *Who Came First* showed. Though Reizner would have been content merely for Pete's blessing, Pete involved himself with the entire recording process during the orchestral *Tommy* sessions. The London Symphony Orchestra was assembled together with a chamber choir and a slew of distinguished names from the rock world including Rod Stewart, Steve Winwood, Maggie Bell, Ringo Starr, Sandy Denny, Graham Bell and Merry Clayton. Also rounded up were Richard Harris and John Entwistle. Roger Daltrey was delighted when Reizner approached him, after first trying Stewart, to sing the title role.

The album was a million-seller and a stage version at London's Rainbow Theatre sold out despite the high cost of tickets. It was a charity event that raised almost ten thousand pounds but Pete was nervous and, playing the part of the narrator, he missed cues, insulted the audience and Reizner. "It brought to life the whole original idea I had for *Rael*," he said. "At last I was to hear something I had written played by a grand orchestra. Later on, particularly after being involved in the live performances of this version, I grew disenchanted with it. It seemed bleak even though it had much that the original never had and it brought *Tommy* to a whole new audience."

Around the same time, Pete had heard of Clapton's plight and after visiting the reclusive guitarist at his Berkshire home proposed a one-off concert at the Rainbow the following January. "Pete did what he did because he couldn't stand so much talent going to waste," wrote Dave Marsh. "Despite whatever pettiness, hypocrisy and terror might befuddle him, there was not a more decent or compassionate man than Townshend in rock."

Pete assembled a band that included guitarist Ronnie Wood, a co-conspirator in the event, Steve Winwood, Rick Grech, Jim Capaldi, Jimmy Karstein and percussionist Rebop Pukwana. Clapton arrived late for the show and his nervousness showed but the night put Clapton on the road to recovery. His gratitude to Pete was profound.

# CHAPTER SEVEN

All had not been well on The Who's business front for some time. The style of management provided by Kit Lambert and Chris Stamp, the stretching of cheques, the snappy ideas, the full tilt promotional thrust that characterised the workings of New Action Ltd., were ideal for the sixties, but in the climate of the seventies, when The Who no longer needed promoting through outrage, when logistical professionalism and sound financial advice was required, the management team was largely redundant.

Peter Rudge now handled all the group's business affairs in America and a new assistant, Bill Curbishley, looked after day to day matters back home. Bill was like Roger, straightforward, down-to-earth, without airs and graces. Bill was also developing into a hard-nosed dealmaker, a skill that Lambert and Stamp had never acquired despite all the questionable moves they played when no one knew where the next pound was coming from.

Roger had never much liked Kit Lambert and when Lambert and Chris Stamp rejected his first solo album, the relationship went into a further spiral. There was an ugly incident with a stopped cheque for monies that were owed to The Who in back royalties. Roger took matters into his own hands and ordered an independent audit of New Action's books. Inevitably there were questions to be answered. Which is not to say that Lambert and Stamp were dishonest. They were simply cavalier in their business dealings and Pete, who with Keith Moon exhibited similar traits, had no wish to sever the connection. The opposing factions lined up and the problem would not go away.

"I know Roger's very conscious all the time of the money set up," said Pete. "I think it's quite simply because he can't sleep at night unless he does actually know what we're earning. But that's probably because he's never spent the way Keith and I have – which is why we don't care how much we've got. We spend what we want to spend and never ask questions later. I've never got into the red because my writing money has kept me a wee bit ahead of the group but Keith has occasionally gone into the red through overspending. But in the end you just say, 'We're just going to have to do a few more tours or something'".

Against this unsettling background, The Who finally went back to work together as a group. The new recording project was one that Pete had been toying with for much of 1972, a new opera based originally on an idea named 'Rock Is Dead – Long Live Rock' but now re-thought out as *Quadrophenia*.

They had decided to build their own studio and inaugurate the premises in Battersea by recording their new album there. Unfortunately, Rampart Studios was far from completed in time and the sessions were done with Ronnie Lane's recently acquired mobile studio parked outside. This far from ideal setup was compounded by the fact that Kit Lambert, assigned by Pete to produce the new work, was incapable of doing the job. Lambert was in a bad way: as The Who's fortunes spiralled, Lambert had gone steadily downhill, abusing himself on drugs and alcohol, and his presence at the *Quadrophenia* sessions was more a liability than an asset.

*Quadrophenia* began life as two songs (*Love Reign O'er Me* and *Is It In My Head*) already recorded with Glyn Johns, never a man to see eye to eye with Lambert, as producer. Pete has claimed that over fifty songs were actually written for this project but only fourteen more were added to the original two to make up the eventual four-sided LP. Initially, it was intended to record the opera in quadrophonic sound but this plan was abandoned as impractical.

At first, the sessions ran reasonably smoothly. "I've really had more control over this album than any other Who album," said Pete. "I directed it, if you like, and certainly people in the band have contributed fantastic amounts in roles that they normally wouldn't play. This is the first Who album when The Who have used each other's capabilities as musicians to the full."

His euphoria was short-lived. Within a few weeks the group became disenchanted with the project for a number of reasons. Roger wasn't happy with the material he'd been given to sing, there wasn't room for a song by John on the record and Keith, normally the character whose explosive drumming sparked The Who's most inspired music, was off form for reasons akin to those that affected Kit Lambert.

"It was a very ambitious co-operative project," said Pete. "I wanted everybody in the group to write their own songs and stuff. Everybody was supposed to engineer their own image. I wanted the group to go in and play a piece of music which was completely spontaneous and then give people their respective segment of the track. As always the band just looked at me like I was crazy and walked away. I've explained it to a lot of people and everybody seems to be able to understand it but them. Then John wrote a song which he wouldn't play for me because he thought it summed up the whole album in one song."

*Quadrophenia* did not end up in the filing cabinet as Lifehouse had done but was completed regardless of confusion and disguised hostility. It is the story of Jimmy the Mod, just out of school, who joins in various Mod activities (Brighton, a Who concert, pills, girls) and comes to the conclusion that he is double schitzophrenic (Quadrophonic in fact). Each side of his four-way personality is supposed to be represented by a member of The Who and each member of The Who has his own theme on the album.

The music which recounts Jimmy's life and problems is grand in the Wagnerian tradition, all sweeping synthesisers, French horns from John and rumbling timpani from Keith, all quite different from the music which The Who had previously released. Unfortunately it was not produced with the clarity of sound that characterised *Who's Next* and neither did Roger have a concrete identity as he did with *Tommy*. While the sweeping majesty of the music (well, most of it) once again camouflaged a vague and to non-English ears incomprehensible, story line, *Quadrophenia* was not so much a Who album as a Pete Townshend project in which The Who played under his direction.

"We get drowned in synthesisers," said Roger. "You'll never get The Who to play like machines. We're not robots. If you want to add musicians then it's not The Who. We've outlasted everyone else because kids want to see The Who, these four people."

The album was finally released in November, 1973, and, predictably, it was an emormous hit. A tour had been planned to coincide with its release, firstly a handful of British dates then a month in America, their first US dates in almost two years. Naturally the music from *Quadrophenia* would occupy the greater proportion of their set.

To perform the new material live required extensive use of backing tapes and extensive rehearsal, but only two days had been set aside before the tour was due to open at Trentham Gardens in Stoke. On the second day of rehearsals frayed tempers exploded and a nasty exchange of abuse between Pete and Roger led to their first fight in almost a decade. Pete bashed Roger on the head with his guitar, John grabbed Pete to prevent the scrap developing, Pete called Roger a "dirty little cunt", Pete threw off John and landed two punches, Roger poleaxed Pete who collapsed out cold, and Keith burst into tears.

"It was a bit of a non-argument," Roger admitted later. "The last thing in the world I wanted to do was to have a fist fight with Pete Townshend. Unfortunately he hit me first with a guitar. I really felt terrible about it afterwards. Pete should never try to be a fighter... I was forced to lay one on him, but it was only one."

The outburst had been simmering for months. Roger was miffed at his role in *Quadrophenia* and still at odds with Pete over the management problems, and Pete was angry over the difficulties caused by using backing tapes and at what he viewed as ingratitude for the work load he had undertaken on

*Above:* In the days before Op Art: The Who appearing on Ready Steady Go! 1965.

*Above:* The Who outside Keith Moon's house, 1973.

*Above and Below:* Tragedy at the Riverfront Coliseum in Cincinnati, December 3, 1979.
*Next page:* Shea Stadium, 1980.

*Left:* The Who at the Cannes Film
Festival, 1982.

*Right:* In New York, 1981.

*Below:* Madison Square Garden.

*Next page:* At JFK Stadium,
Philadelphia.

Below: The Rolling Stones Rock and Roll Circus.

the group's behalf.

Pete was revived in hospital but suffered temporary loss of memory. No worse start to a Who tour could be imagined.

After the first show at Stoke, five *Quadrophenia* numbers were dropped but the over reliance on backing tapes was only part of the problem. Roger felt it necessary to explain the story line of *Quadrophenia* between songs and this had an unsettling affect on the pacing of the show. Pete thought the explanations were unnecessary anyway. "I think the story line isn't so complicated that it bears explaining. A kid sits on a rock and remembers the things that have happened to him in the last few days. I think if you explain the story line too much it demeans the music, makes it too Tanglewood Tales. The story, after all, is just a peg to hang ideas on. When Roger gets too literal about the story I have to cut it and make it lighter."

"The thing we did on *Quadrophenia*," retorted Roger, "was that we bullshitted it up so much there was nothing left for the kids to think about. It was done for them."

The tour itself fared no better than the recording or rehearsal sessions. After a few shakey shows in Stoke, Wolverhampton and Manchester, the tapes malfunctioned seriously at Newcastle City Hall. Fifty minutes into the show, during *5.15*, perhaps *Quadrophenia's* best song, Pete went berserk when the tape failed to synchronise with the group. He grabbed sound engineer Bobby Pridden by the neck, pulled him sprawling into centre stage, and proceeded to demolish the piles of tapes and playback equipment. The band watched in disbelief, then followed Pete off stage and waited while tempers cooled.

Half an hour later the band re-emerged to play a set of old favourites and even the much abused Pridden was back behind the mixing desk. Pete apologised and the next day Pridden went out and bought him a new guitar. "We had no money and I had to buy a guitar out of my own pocket to keep the flag flying," Pridden told Richard Barnes. "And the old chap (Pete) is on the phone saying, 'Do you need a hand down there, Bob?'. I understand it. If I didn't I wouldn't have been there with them all those years."

The American tour that followed was no more successful. On

the opening night in San Francisco, Keith Moon collapsed over his drum kit after a ragged *Quadrophenia* and was eventually replaced by a drummer from the audience. Keith was back behind his kit for two Los Angeles shows that followed but as the tour crossed America eastwards, the shows became more and more frustrating and the on stage hostility between Roger and Pete never abated. Since their were no Mods in America and *Quadrophenia* was essentially a Mod experience, the audiences were as baffled by the music as they were by the hostility of the performers. The great cheers that greeted familiar material were like arrows plunged deep into Pete's heart.

In Montreal, the entire group wound up in jail after a hotel wrecking incident inspired by Keith Moon and escalated by Pete. Pete wound up sharing a cell with Roger, who was furious because he'd retired to bed early and hadn't been involved in the demolition. They were released the following morning on three thousand dollars bail and only just made Boston in time for that night's shows.

The American tour closed in Washington DC on December 6 and back in London, The Who performed four *Quadrophenia* shows in the week before Christmas at the Edmonton Sundown. The following February, three *Quad* shows were undertaken in France after which the tapes were packed away for good. No one was sorry to see the back of them.

Plans to make a film of *Tommy* had been simmering since the release of the album in 1969. Kit Lambert had shopped around for finance without success and his inability to strike a deal was yet another factor in the decline of his relationship with The Who. Universal Pictures, who owned MCA Records, had first refusal on the production but they rejected Lambert's script and dropped the option in 1971. Other prospectors panned the river without success.

"We went through a whole thing when what we were really after was a deal which would enable us to control the film," said Pete. "But we could never get close to that. Film companies always wanted somebody else to control it."

Pete found himself being courted by movie moguls to whom

the spiritual aspects of the property were of zero consequence. "What's happened is that an American director has taken me to lunch, sat me down and said, 'You know, Pete, we're talking about a million dollar movie here, and what we wanna know is your thoughts, we wanna know how you wanna make the movie, Pete.' What they were really saying was, 'Okay, you little English poof, you make the film and please make it gross six times as much as the album did.' And I'd sit there and tell them how to make it. Then they'd go away and decide it wasn't such a good idea after all. Then a week later another mogul would come over and take me out to lunch."

Eventually Robert Stigwood became involved in the deal. Back in the sixties Stigwood had helped The Who by allowing them to release records on his Reaction label during the dispute with Shel Talmy. He had once been The Who's booking agent, was a long-standing friend of Lambert and Stamp, and, in the intervening years, had prospered enormously through a wide range of interests in the music and entertainment industry. He was also the manager of Pete's pal, Eric Clapton.

Stigwood put together a deal with Columbia Pictures and arranged for Ken Russell, a director long admired by Pete, to work on the film and produce a script. Unfortunately Pete found himself drawn into the production of the film more than he would have liked. At first he turned down the job of musical director but when Stigwood insisted (and upped his fee from one hundred thousand dollars to one hundred thousand pounds), Pete agreed.

"I quite liked the opportunity of having a bash at the music again. I felt it had been short-changed the first time," he told Richard Barnes. "The only thing was I went right over the top, trying to improve it and show some of the compositions were good and because they had been short-changed by the original production, I tended to over-produce – loads and loads of synthesiser on everything. I wouldn't let anything go by without covering it with synthesiser and lots of clever introductions to cross-themes and things like that. In other words, all those overdubs that were denied on the first album, I was making up for on the *Tommy* film."

The workload was colossal, mainly because Russell decided that the entire script should be sung and that many of the singers were unable to sing. Pete had suggested a number of excellent singers for various roles (Cleo Laine, Georgia Brown, Arthur Brown) but his ideas were overruled by Russell and instead the main parts were taken by Oliver Reed, Ann-Margret and Jack Nicholson. Roger Daltrey was happy to play Tommy, though David Essex was also considered, and Elton John took the part of the Pinball Wizard. Keith Moon was ideally suited to the role of Uncle Ernie, the self-confessed pervert, and Tina Turner became an inspired Acid Queen.

"With Ken Russell I was prepared to make concessions and compromise some points in order to have Ken make his alterations," Pete told Richard Barnes. "It just meant another evolution of the concept. I told him I didn't care if he altered all the words if he needed to."

The re-recording of *Tommy* was done at Rampart Studios or Pete's home base at Twickenham during the first half of 1974. When this was completed the tracks had to be dubbed onto film and synchronised, a tedious and painstaking job which Pete accomplished less than willingly. Though he no longer used drugs, he began to drink brandy in quantities that rivalled Keith Moon. His hair began to fall out and when he visited a specialist to have his hearing checked, the doctor warned him that performing live with The Who could damage his ears permanently.

Various isolated Who shows had been planned including an outdoor appearance at the Charlton Athletic Football ground in South London and a four-night stint in New York at Madison Square Garden. Also looming was a solo appearance at The Roundhouse in Camden Town, a charity event which Pete had agreed to play after a casual inquiry appealed to his charitable instincts. Aside from performing privately at a few Baba meetings, Pete had never appeared solo before and much to his distaste, the Camden appearance was blown out of all proportion when the music press got hold of the story. There were even reports that US Who fans were preparing to fly over to London specially for it; Pete was terrified.

"I did that after the *Tommy* film recording sessions so I was still pretty shattered. I'd just overcommitted myself again," he told Richard Barnes. "I'd said to Lisa Strike, one of the singers on the *Tommy* film, 'Oh yeah, I'll do the Roundhouse for you' and thought it was going to be a very small thing but it turned out to be bloody massive.

"People were ringing me up and saying, 'I hear you're doing a solo gig at the Roundhouse' and I thought, 'Hold on, this is getting out of control'. I started to work seven days a week before the gig trying to get material together to make it better, so that by the time I came to do the gig, I'd actually been doing it for about a week before up in my studio.'

Pete didn't eat for three days before the show on April 14. When he did appear, the nerves vanished and he acquitted himself well despite a drunken heckler. Using electric and acoustic guitars, keyboards, synthesiser tapes and various special effects, he ran through a set that included *Pinball Wizard*, *The Seeker*, Jimmy Reed's *Big Boss Man* and *My Generation*. All monies received went towards a coach for the Camden Square Community Play Centre.

A month later Pete appeared with The Who at Charlton. They had abandoned *Quadrophenia*, retaining just two songs *5.15* and *The Punk Meets The Godfather*, and settled on a set that stretched back through the past. Unfortunately, the weather was atrocious and Pete was depressed at the crowd's passive acceptance of what he considered to be a mediocre performance by the group. The group had not played together since the three French *Quadrophenia* concerts in February, yet it was only Pete who complained about their lack of cohesion. Worse was to come.

In mid-June, The Who were scheduled to play four shows at Madison Square Garden. New York had been missed during the American *Quadrophenia* dates and this short season (at which they broke the existing record for consecutive appearances at the venue) was widely seen as the highlight of the city's rock year. All eighty thousand tickets sold out within hours of a single radio announcement.

Pete was in a depressive spiral when he checked into the Pierre

Hotel on Fifth Avenue at the beginning of the week. He'd been on the wagon for a few days and was sober at the Garden rehearsals but on the opening night things started to go wrong. Equipment malfunctioned, unwanted squeaks belched forth and the PA sound, which in the past had been as crisp as anyone's, was muggy and stilted.

Pete yelled at Bob Pridden but nothing came right; perhaps he wouldn't have minded so much if the audience hadn't lapped up the show anyway; worse than that, they commanded Pete to jump ("as if I was Pavlov's dog", he said later). His legs gave way beneath him and all the twists and turns, the kicks and spins, seemed for the first time ever to be an impossible burden.

"In all the years I'd been with The Who I'd never had to force myself," he told Nik Cohn. "All the leaping about and guitar smashing, even though I'd done it a thousand times, it was always totally natural. And then, on the first night at the Garden, I suddenly lost it. I didn't know what I was doing there, stuck up on stage in front of all these people. I had no instinct left; I had to do it from memory. So I looked down into the front row and all these kids were squealing 'Jump, jump, jump.' And I panicked... I was lost.

"It was the most incredible feeling. After half my lifetime to suddenly go blank. The other three shows I was terrified. I got smashed or I couldn't have gone on."

For the remainder of the week Pete submerged himself in brandy, stayed out most of the night clubbing with Keith and John and joined in heated disputes backstage. All the shows were below par. The fans in the front few rows, many of whom saw every show, were faces Pete recognised from earlier classic New York appearances, faces that brought back memories of the Murray The K shows in 1967, the Fillmore in 1969 and the Met in 1970. "When my drunken legs gave way under me, as I tried to do a basic cliché leap and shuffle, a few loving fans got up a chant. 'Jump! Jump! Jump!'", Pete wrote in a 1977 Rolling Stone piece.

Back in London, filled with misery, Pete completed work on the *Tommy* soundtrack, convinced that The Who would never perform live again.

# CHAPTER EIGHT

Pete had neither the songs nor the enthusiasm to provide The Who with material for an original album in 1974. Instead they released *Odds And Sods*, the collection of interesting out-takes that John Entwistle compiled from leftover material, much of it from the aborted Lifehouse project.

The Who were in disarray. Keith Moon, separated from his wife and soon to be divorced, now lived in California; Entwistle, restless from the lack of live performance, was making plans to put his own band together; Roger Daltrey, too, wanted to resume live work but Pete was in no state to tour. Knee-deep in the arduous *Tommy* film soundtrack and unable to rationalise the onset of middle age with playing in a rock 'n' roll band, he retreated to the studio where empty Remy Martin bottles lay stacked up against the pile of tapes that always seemed to need re-mixing.

The conflict with Kit Lambert and Chris Stamp had come to a head. When Pete discovered that almost half a million pounds of his publishing money had gone astray he finally sided with Roger and, along with Entwistle, sued the renegade pair for mismanagement. Bill Curbishley took over officially as manager of The Who in the summer of 1974, but the immediate result of these legal proceedings was to tie up The Who's record royalties until a judgement could be reached. Their only source of income, therefore, was from live appearances.

The razzmatazz that surrounded the release of the *Tommy* film in March 1975 depressed Pete still further. Lavish premiére

103

parties hosted by gimmick-conscious Hollywood publicists and attended by drag queens and gossip column regulars were anathema to all of Pete's worthy ideals, the "sell out" he'd strained so hard to avoid. The film was a vehicle for Roger who came through with flying colours; for Pete it was one more step along the road to misery.

On May 19, 1975, Pete turned thirty. That week he poured out his heart to Roy Carr of the New Musical Express. In a brutally frank interview he criticised other rock musicians, The Who, the state of rock and its audience, anything and everything that had been plaguing him for the past twelve months. As he warmed to the subject, Pete uttered exaggerations galore but the published piece set the stage for a public slanging match with Roger Daltrey.

"I really hate feeling too old to be doing what I'm doing," he told Carr – and this theme was reiterated throughout. "It's just that when I'm standing there on stage playing rock 'n' roll, I often feel I'm too old for it. When Roger speaks about 'we'll all be rocking in our wheelchairs' he might be but you won't catch me rockin' in no wheelchair. I don't think it's possible. I might be making music in a wheelchair – maybe even with The Who – but I feel that The Who have got to realise that the things we're gonna be writing about and singing about are rapidly changing. The group as a whole have got to realise that they are not the same group that they used to be."

Avoiding the finality of a blunt declaration that The Who were over the hill, Pete nevertheless dwelt on the problems that all successful groups encounter after staying together for a number of years. "Forget that tired old myth that rock 'n' roll is just making records, pullin' birds, gettin' pissed and having a good time. That's not what it's all about. And I don't think Roger really believes that either. I think that's what he'd really like to believe rock 'n' roll to be all about.

"There is no point to your life when you can stop working. You can't suddenly turn round and say, 'we're on the crest of a wave so now it's time to sit back and boogie'. Deep down inside everyone wants to do this but it's tantamount to retiring altogether."

Pete explained why almost eighteen months had elapsed since the release of a new album of Who material. "At the moment what governs the speed of The Who is the diversification of individual interests. We would have been recording a new album much earlier were it not for the fact that Roger is making another film with Ken Russell.

"Roger chose to make the film and John wanted to tour with his own band The Ox so I've been working on tracks for my next solo album. Invariably, what will happen is that once we all get into the studio, I'll think 'Oh fuck it' and I'll play Roger, John and Keith the tracks I've been keeping for my own album and they'll pick the best. So long as The Who exists I'll never get the pick of my own material... and that's what I dream of."

Whatever frustration this may have caused, Pete nevertheless hedged his bets. "But if The Who ever broke up because the material was substandard then I'd really kick myself.

"However much of a bastard it is to get everyone together in a recording studio, things eventually turn out allright. You see, though it has never been important in the past, we do have this problem that everyone has been engaged on their own project, so that the separate social existence that we lead has become even more acute. I mean, I just couldn't live without Moonie and if I could go over to the States and spend a couple of months with him we'd probably a lot closer. As it happens I haven't seen Keith since last August (actually they met at the *Tommy* film premieres in March). I may have seen a lot more of John but as yet I haven't seen his new group or listened properly to his album because apart from working on *Tommy* I've been putting together new material.

"And the same thing applies to Roger: as soon as someone decides to do something outside The Who the pressure suddenly ceases, because they are the people who put the pressure on me. Let me make this clear: I don't put pressure on them. I don't say 'we've got to get into the studio this very minute because I've got these songs that I've just gotta get off my chest'. It's always been the other way around. They always rush up to me and insist that we've got to cut a new album and get back on the road."

Pete went on to criticise other rock performers, Mick Jagger, Steve Marriott, Chuck Berry, Jeff Beck, Jimmy Page and Yes, and The Who themselves came in for a tongue lashing. "When we were gigging in this country at the early part of last year I was thoroughly depressed. I honestly felt The Who were going on stage every night and, for the sake of the die-hard fans, copying what The Who used to be."

The interview closed with Pete again recounting the frustrations he had felt during The Who's concerts at Madison Square Garden the previous year, clearly an episode that ignited his depression. "Perhaps the reason why so many young kids can still get into The Who is simply because it's a very zesty, athletic performance. However if we just restricted our gigs to performing songs that we'd just written yesterday and ignored all the old material then I'm positive that we'd really narrow down our audience tremendously.

"All I know is that when we last played Madison Square Garden I felt acute shades of nostalgia. All The Who freaks had crowded round the front of the stage and when I gazed into the audience all I could see were the very same sad faces that I'd seen at every New York Who gig. There was about a thousand of them and they turned up for every bloody show at the Garden as if it were some Big Event – The Who triumph over New York. It was like some bicentennial celebration and *they* were there to share in the glory of it all.

"*They* hadn't come to watch The Who, but to let everyone know *they* were the original Who fans. *They* had followed us from the very beginning and it was *their* right.

"It was dreadful. They were telling us what to play. Every time I tried to make an announcement they all yelled out 'Shut up Townshend and let Entwistle play *Boris The Spider*', and if that wasn't bad enough, during other songs they'd all start chanting 'jump… jump… jump… jump… jump…'

"I was so brought down by it all. Is this what it had all degenerated into?"

The Who finally re-assembled to make music together during June and July at Rampart Studios. These were the sessions that produced *The Who By Numbers* and, in the interests of greater

106

efficiency, both Pete and Keith stopped drinking – at least temporarily. Pete's outburst in NME was not mentioned though Roger, who resented his criticism the most, was fighting back an urge to reply.

The opportunity arrived in August. During an interview with NME's Tony Stewart, ostensibly to promote his second solo album *Ride A Rock Horse*, Roger hit back at Pete's remarks with all the venom he could muster.

"I've never read such a load of bullshit in my life," he said. "To be perfectly honest it really took a lot of my Who energy out reading that. I don't feel that way about The Who, about our audiences or anything in that way. I've talked to fans and I think Townshend lost a lot of respect from that article. He's talked himself up his own ass. Pete Townshend didn't die before he got old. Yet death isn't his problem, it's the passing of the years and his current position in what he feels is a young man's occupation.

"My main criticism is the generalisation that The Who were bad. They weren't bad. I think we've had a few gigs where Townshend was bad... and I'll go on record as saying that. We could have done Madison Square Garden with our eyes closed, only the group was running on three cylinders, especially the last night. You don't generalise and say The Who was bad... wasn't quite as good as we could have been, but it was because Townshend was in a bad frame of mind about what he wanted to do. And he didn't play well. Sure, we all have our off nights, but don't go around saying The Who were bad."

Roger particularly resented Pete's allegation that rock 'n' roll was to him 'making records, pulling birds, getting pissed and having a good time'. "That just shows he doesn't understand me at all," said the man who had now sung Pete's songs for a decade. "The naiveté of that is that the last few bad gigs The Who did were, in my opinion, apart from his head trip, bad because they were physically out boozing and balling all night. And by the time they got to the show at night they were physically incapable of doing a good show. That was Townshend. Moon does it but he can control it. On the last few gigs Townshend was pissed and incapable."

Roger's final thrust was direct and to the point. "Don't talk to me about booze because I've never been on stage drunk in the last seven years, Mr Townshend. I don't know if you've ever noticed, maybe he hasn't, but I have. I remember every show we've ever done. I'm just getting a bit fed up with these left-handed attacks.

"One of the sad things is that Pete and I are probably never going to be able to communicate. I think I'll have to sit down and write a letter to the band, because there's no way of ever speaking to them about it."

No other group, ever, had used the music press in this way; to speak out on matters they felt unable to discuss between themselves. The yawning chasm that separated Pete Townshend from Roger Daltrey, the difference in temperaments, ambitions, politics, spiritual outlook and general philosophy, was as wide in 1975 as it had been in 1965. Their joint achievements had done nothing to close the gap. Yet Pete needed Roger as much as Roger needed Pete and both knew that The Who was bigger than both of them.

Somehow, despite it all, the group stayed together.

Many of the songs on *The Who By Numbers* could have been written for a solo album by Pete. His paranoia over age and disillusionment was rampant in the lyrics while the music called for a lighter approach than The Who's traditional style dictated. Several tracks (*However Much I Booze*, *In A Hand Or A Face* and *How Many Friends*) were explicitly linked with Pete's anxieties and even John Entwistle's track *Success Story* echoed similar fears.

Unlike *Quadrophenia* or *Who's Next*, the new album contained no synthesisers. Missing also were Pete's block chords, the whiplash guitar style that characterised so many of his songs. Its most gentle track, *Blue Red And Grey*, was a Townshend solo of haunting irony in which the singer movingly recounts his disenchantment with a jet-set lifestyle.

"It was an extremely effective record in putting across what was in my head at the time," said Pete. "And I think to some extent it was what was really happening to the band at the time too.

"It was revealing, I suppose, because it was all I had left at the time. I just thought 'What am I going to do, because I'm fucked up, not writing anything?'. There's one little chink in the armour, and that's the ukelele track (*Blue, Red And Grey*)."

Whatever the background to recording the album, *The Who By Numbers* was a predictable commercial success and *Squeeze Box* ("A devastatingly simple song", said Pete) was the group's first hit single since *Won't Get Fooled Again*. The songs did not translate well on stage, however, and only two songs, *Squeeze Box* and *Dreaming From The Waist*, would be featured in forthcoming live performances.

In August, when the *Numbers* sessions were over, Pete flew to America with his family to spend a month visiting friends and fellow Baba lovers. Much of the time was spent at Myrtle Beach, South Carolina, the site of a large Baba centre; and in Northern California at the home of Murshida Duce, who headed a Baba-orientated Sufi cult. For some time Pete had intended to open a Meher Baba centre in London and he sought guidance from fellow devotees, often expressing the view that his life as a rock star was incompatible with that of a Baba lover.

At one point in the trip Pete virtually broke down in front of Murshida Duce. He spoke at length about his insecurities with The Who and, treating the interview as a confessional, rambled on about the excesses of life in rock 'n' roll. "Without batting an eyelid," Pete revealed later, "she listened to stuff that was making me recoil myself, then went on to talk about her own life. In short, she got me right in perspective."

Pete also revealed that at one point in the visit he received a message from the Almighty. "Keep playing guitar with The Who until further notice," it said.

Spiritually refreshed, he returned to London and began rehearsals for The Who's first concert tour in two years. Keith Moon noted that Pete had a smile on his face when he walked into the rehearsal, a welcome omen for the gruelling schedule ahead. Despite Pete's fears over the group becoming a "golden oldies" band, the programme selected included early singles (*I Can't Explain, Substitute, Magic Bus* and *My Generation*), a half hour *Tommy* medley, four songs from *Who's Next* (*Baba O'Riley,*

*My Wife, Behind Blue Eyes* and *Won't Get Fooled Again*) and the two new songs from *The Who By Numbers*. Apparently Pete had temporarily exorcised his frustration over repetition.

The new album was released in October on the Polydor label, an indication that the group's relationship with Kit Lambert and Chris Stamp and their jointly-owned Track Records was now over. Lambert, by this time, had taken complete leave of his senses and issued a mindless press release indicating his intention to sue Robert Stigwood (as producer of the *Tommy* film) and fire both Bill Curbishley and Chris Stamp. It was all hot air, of course, for Lambert was careering downhill fast: hopelessly alcoholic, intermittently addicted to heroin, Kit lived mostly in Venice where he acquired a palazzo and chased young Italian boys.

The British leg of the new Who tour opened at Stoke-On-Trent on October 4 and from the opening bars of *I Can't Explain*, it was clear that Roger Daltrey's professional instincts had triumphed over Pete's pessimism. Like their peers in the top league, The Who were now a smooth-running machine, perhaps the smoothest running of all, but still a machine. Each song was rattled off with consummate skill, each gesture was retained and respected, and to cap it all, there was a staggering laser display which enhanced Roger's presence all the more.

The fans were satisfied and so were Roger, John and Keith. Pete diplomatically kept his mouth shut and performed each night as Pavlov's dog might have performed, jumping and kicking, spinning and twisting as he always had. He was still, and always would be, the most visual guitarist in rock and sometimes, when the mood took him, he even cracked a guitar for old times' sake. Ideals had been buried beneath the enormous grosses.

The British dates climaxed with four sell-out shows at Wembley's Empire Pool and were followed by shows in Holland and Germany. The first leg of a three section US tour opened at the Summit Houston on November 20 and, according to Variety Magazine, netted just over three million dollars. Included in the US itinerary was a show at the seventy-eight thousand capacity Pontiac Stadium near Detroit which earned

110

them six hundred thousand dollars. The three week swing closed at the Spectrum in Philadelphia where Pete wrecked two guitars, one midway through the set. Bristling with self-confidence, as tight as they had ever been thanks to the non-stop road work, The Who finished 1975 with three shows at Hammersmith Odeon and spent the first two months of 1976 recuperating before another round of concerts in Europe and America.

The 1975/6 tour series was the most gruelling schedule since 1971, and not until they reached America for another three-week blitz in March did any problems arise. Then, at the opening show in Boston Gardens, Keith Moon collapsed and the concert was abandoned with promises of a make-up date later in the tour.

In many respects, Keith Moon was like Pete Townshend. Both strongly identified with the lyrics of *My Generation*, revelling in excess, unwilling to recognise maturity, but while Pete struggled to come to terms with adulthood, Keith simply looked the other way. Roger Daltrey and John Entwistle had no such problems and when Moon's behaviour affected his drumming and the professionalism of the group – as it now did – they entertained the thought that another drummer could be found. Pete, on the other, dismissed the idea.

In late May, The Who performed three big outdoor dates at football stadiums in London, Glasgow and Swansea. The sound level at the first was measured at one hundred and twenty decibels, sufficient to gain a mention in the Guinness Book of Records as the loudest performance ever by a rock group.

The touring continued intermittently until October with shows
in the American south, the West Coast and Canada. A concert in the Gator Bowl at Jacksonville, which was sparsely attended by Who standards, prompted Pete to remark that, "we were playing for the people who weren't there". In Oakland they shared top billing with The Grateful Dead, a curious pairing with nostalgic overtones far removed from Pete's ideals.

The final show was in Toronto, at Maple Leaf Gardens, on October 21. Pete wrecked a Les Paul guitar and Keith stumbled through a drum kit that would never again be used in America.

# CHAPTER NINE

After the 1976 tours, Pete returned to his Twickenham home with
a feeling that his obligations to The Who and their fans had been discharged. No further concerts had been scheduled for the remainder of that year and neither was any live work planned for 1977. The arrangement suited him perfectly.

One reason why he was reluctant to tour was the persistent ringing in his ears and a doctor's warning that further punishment might do irreparable damage to his hearing. Another was that family life was suffering through being away from home too often.

"I made a conscious decision that my first love, The Who, would in future take second place to my real love – my wife and my daughters," he said. "When I got home from one of the American tours I wanted to return home as a conquering hero because it had been a marvellous tour for us. But when I got to the front door steps I wasn't the hero. I walked back to the kids who didn't even know who I was. They were very cagey and intimidated by me. They were even perplexed because I wore an American sea captain's uniform which I'd bought in Chicago. I can see their faces still.

"Our marriage staggered on for a while but then came a showdown. My old lady just broke down one day and said she'd run out of energy and that was it. It dawned on me that what she was really saying was, 'I don't really love you. I don't care whether you go away or whether you stay. I don't give a damn about you or your life, or the way you don't think about us'. I went away for two days and thought about all she had said. I saw the truth… that if I lost Karen and the family I wouldn't be able to face life at all. What's more, I wouldn't be able to do anything for The Who either.

"There were things I got from The Who that nobody could ever get from a marriage partnership. But on the other hand what really made me a human being was my relationship with my old lady. I knew that's what I needed to preserve most. From that point of view my family became my first priority. I had to show Karen that I loved her and spend my time trying to convince people to buy records. Some people who are heavily into The Who felt this was a great snub on my part because, in effect, I was telling them, 'Listen, you're not as important as my family'. Fortunately others understood my predicament."

Thus resolved, Pete settled into the role of family man and rediscovered the joys of home life. He would have been happy to forget The Who still existed.

Towards the end of 1976 there appeared on the British charts a song called *Anarchy In The UK*. Bereft of melody or musical discipline yet sizzling with energy and malevolence, it heralded the arrival of punk rock and what came to be known as new wave music. The Sex Pistols created a new generation gap, the gap between groups like The Who and groups like themselves and countless others inspired to knock the sterile establishmentarianism that was rampant in the music scene.

To the punk bands and their followers, The Who and their peers were boring old farts, redundant veterans trading on former accomplishments long forgotten and largely despised. Their motive was to bring down the established order; in this they failed, but the changes they brought about were important and far-reaching. The stranglehold of the major record companies was broken by a stream of sassy independents, and the closed shop mentality, in which virtuoso musicians thrived, was put to rout.

Most of the established superstar bands loathed the punks but Pete Townshend and, to a lesser degree, the rest of The Who welcomed them. In many respects the punks were a reflection

113

of their earlier selves – arrogant, idealistic, uncompromising and, above all, an awesome sight to behold on stage.

The punks' basic premise – that rock 'n' roll was a young person's game – was exactly the same as that which had troubled Pete's conscience for the past three years. "Despite the fact that The Who do go on and on, one of the things that had driven us on and on is that we've looked around and said, 'Who is there to pick up the glove?'," said Pete. "There was nobody… now there is.

"I used to wake up in the night praying to be destroyed. Get me out of this bloody whirlpool, I thought. In the end I actually thought of inventing a new form of music which would take over from where The Who left off. In my imagination I invented punk rock a thousand times. I thought the hypocrisy of the position we were in was just unbelievable. 'Where are the young people of today?' I thought. 'Where are their heroes of today?'".

It was during the height of the Sex Pistols' notoriety, in March of 1977, that a final settlement was reached in the litigation between The Who and their former managers, Kit Lambert and Chris Stamp. One stumbling block had been a dispute over Pete's American publishing royalties and after much wheeling and dealing, in which Allan Klein acted as an intermediary, Pete agreed to accept one million dollars in full settlement of his US copyrights and a further six figure sum in back royalty payments. All rights now reverted to The Who's new companies and litigation was henceforth dropped.

Clutching a cheque for seven figures, Pete left the final meeting in a fragile, unhinged state and, with Chris Stamp in tow, headed for the Speakeasy Club near Oxford Circus where John Otway and Wild Willy Barrett were appearing. Two drinks later he was ranting and raving to anyone who would listen, pouring out his guilt at having ditched Kit Lambert for money, at becoming embroiled in business matters he loathed, at anything and everything that now plagued his troubled conscience.

In the gloom he chanced upon two punks whom Stamp identified as members of The Sex Pistols. "What the fuck are

114

you doing in a piss 'ole like this," he demanded, assuming that one or the other of the pair was Johnny Rotten, the leading Pistol and, at the time, the most notorious rock personality in the land.

But Pete was mistaken. The two Pistols were Paul Cook and Steve Jones and when they identified themselves, Pete was further enraged at having failed to expose Rotten in a club where established rock performers, the boring old farts he so obviously despised, had drowned their sorrows for a decade.

"Rock 'n' roll's going down the pan," Pete shouted. "You've got to take over where The Who left off – and this time you've got to finish the fucking job." Warming to his frenzied sermon, Pete mouthed on about decadence and dissillusionment and, to illustrate his tortured sincerity, took out the cheque that weighed so heavily on his mind. Instantly it was ripped to shreds, trodden into the ground and spat upon.

Paul Cook, shrinking from this tirade and clearly under the impression that he was about to be assaulted by a raving lunatic, hesitantly inquired whether this meant that The Who had broken up.

"What does it matter if The Who break up?" yelled Pete. "We're fucking finished.. it's a disaster! We've compromised everything to bits. We're fucking prostitutes."

At this, Cook looked downcast. "We really like The Who, don't we Steve?," he confessed. "They're our favourite group… be a drag if they broke up."

This was too much for Pete. With a mighty scream he left the club and stumbled drunkenly into the night. A nearby shop doorway claimed him and there he lay comatose until a strolling policeman disturbed his sleep in the dawn sunlight. Nursing a twenty-four-carat hangover, he took the early morning tube to Richmond and a taxi to Twickenham where Karen waited impatiently.

"I've been to hell," he said, and crawled into bed.

Fate has been less than kind to Ronnie Lane. When his group The Small Faces called it a day in 1969, their record company went bankrupt and there's a story about their management, perhaps apocryphal, that seems to sum up their unquestioning attitude towards the rewards that fame can bring.

When Ian McLagan first replaced Jimmy Winston on keyboards he was given to understand that the job was offered on a trial basis for which he would receive thirty pounds a week. After three months of satisfactory service he inquired whether the position was now permanent and, if so, whether he was therefore entitled to the same money as the rest of the band. Sure, he was told, and at the end of the following week his pay packet contained twenty-five pounds.

Though Lane profited from the Rod Stewart-led Faces he was in perpetual conflict with Stewart over the inclusion of his own material on their records. After four years he quit, another victim of disillusionment anxious to tone down his lifestyle and ambition. Like Pete Townshend, he became a follower of Meher Baba but his subsequent musical endeavours, which at one time involved performing in a circus-styled big top, cost considerably more than they could ever hope to recoup. By 1976, he was in serious financial trouble.

"I was having a brain trauma at the time," Ronnie told Chris Welch. "I needed to have a talk with Peter about certain things that were going on, and out of it came this album."

The album was *Rough Mix*, the Townshend-Lane collaboration recorded in late 1976 and early 1977.

Original plans called for joint compositions but the finished product contained just one track, an instrumental, where the writing credits were shared. For reasons of temperament the two songwriters produced their music independently. "We tried to do things together to an extent but I think it was more my failing than Ron's," said Pete.

"Having sat and written with Steve Marriott I'm sure he could write with anybody, but I never have. I've never written anything with anybody else. I've taken other people's lyrics and set them to music and I've sometimes worked on other people's songs, but I've never written with anybody because I write unconsciously and tend to just let it spill out. And if anybody says, 'Why don't you change so-and-so', I don't know how to approach it. Because I haven't put it together in an intellectual way, it feels like being caught out. It's almost like

116

having a ghost writer that writes everything for you.

"As far as Ronnie's stuff was concerned I really enjoyed working on them. But his contribution to my songs was much, much deeper. It's hard to explain. For a start, I don't think I would have done the album or the kind of material I did if it were not for Ronnie's encouragement. And that hasn't just started with this album. It has been constant. Ronnie's been one of the few people that I've played demos to and he has always encouraged me to do stuff away from the mainstream of Who clichés."

The album was produced by Glyn Johns who rounded up an all-star team of session players: Eric Clapton, Charlie Watts, John 'Rabbit' Bundrick, John Entwistle, Mel Collins, Henry Spinetti, unofficial Stones keyboard player Ian Stewart and fellow Baba lover Billy Nicholls.

Pete contributed five new songs to the album, three of which stand alongside the best work of his career: *My Baby Gives It Away*, a straight-ahead rock hook; *Keep Me Turning*, a spiritual beat ballad; and *Misunderstood*, a gentle put down of male machismo. All three are performed with a glowing grace quite unlike the staccato jerks that characterise his Who material.

A fourth song, *Street In The City*, was based on an elaborate and rather formal string arrangement conducted by Edwin Astley, his father-in-law.

Lane was no slouch either. He duetted with Pete on the fifth Townshend song *Heart To Hang On To* and a version of Don Williams' country number *Till The Rivers All Run Dry*, and his own song *Annie*, a folkish ballad, was perhaps the most moving track on the entire LP.

*Rough Mix* gathered justifiably excellent reviews and was a brisk seller in the autumn of 1977, the most successful extracurricular Who project thus far.

Twelve months on from their last concert appearance The Who
still had no plans to tour. Pete was adamantly against going on the road and so, to his immense relief, was Roger Daltrey. Having finally extended his profile outside the group, Roger was keen to pursue a career in acting and, together with reformed convict John McVicar, was working on a film project

117

based on the latter's life. Keith Moon, too, was in no state to tour: his drinking was now wildly out of hand, he was overweight and in no physical shape to play drums night after night. Only John Entwistle demurred.

As a business corporation The Who were involved in other matters. Part of the money they'd received from the *Tommy* film had been invested in Shepperton Studios near Staines and the property included rehearsal space, sound stages and buildings to store the colossal array of equipment they'd amassed over the years. Both the space and equipment were rented out to other groups and their two stalwart crewmen, Bob Pridden and John Wolff, were given workshops in which to experiment on sound and lights.

The group were also keen to get a foothold in the movie business and to this end they employed an American Who fanatic called Jeff Stein to research old footage of the band for a Who bio-pic which eventually became *The Kids Are Alright*. Director Frank Roddam was brought in to make a film of *Quadrophenia* and Pete talked seriously of reviving Lifehouse though nothing ever came of it.

Bill Curbishley was the guiding hand behind these ventures. For the first time in their career The Who were managed by a tough and honest businessman, neither an artistic dilettante nor financial delinquent. Lambert and Stamp (and, to a lesser degree Pete Meaden before them) had been creative managers and, as such, were appealing to Pete Townshend in ways that transcended Roger Daltrey's business-like attitude. Curbishley, however, was Roger's man: down to earth, rational and hard-nosed. Pete had little in common with Bill yet, as Dave Marsh had pointed out, Bill "delivered more of Townshend's dream than Kit and Chris had ever been able to do. The Who had their own films in production at last."

In December of 1977 the group went into Rampart Studios to work on a new album with Glyn Johns. Little was achieved. Part of the problem was that Pete's new songs were unsuited to The Who's usual style but of greater import was Keith Moon's wild intemperance and consequent inability to perform with anything like the skill he once displayed. The sessions

118

generally descended into drinking bouts and Roger, when he did turn up, often drove back to his country home in disgust.

"At about six o'clock the port would come out and they'd all start sitting around talking about the old days and telling jokes until it was time to go home," said Jon Astley, Pete's brother-in-law, who was now Glyn John's assistant. "Glyn would often get really bored with the lack of progress and get up and leave."

"Keith was normally incredibly consistent and easily had enough stamina to keep up a powerful rhythm throughout a long number but he seemed to have lost it," wrote Richard Barnes. "He was flagging and losing count. They did take after take and were not getting very far. He'd put on a lot of weight and his sheer physical size slowed him down."

Pete was anxious to change the direction of The Who's music (one of the new songs he'd written was actually called *Music Must Change*) and, because of the punk upheaval, he felt that The Who need no longer be tied down to straightforward rock 'n' roll.

"I'm keen on trying to steer The Who in the direction of doing grandiose projects of some sort," he said. "It would be easy pickings to stick out a hard-edged rock album which would sell a couple of million in the States but, frankly, I'd prefer to make a film, despite the fact that my hair fell out when we did *Tommy*."

The sessions broke up in mid-December and just before Christmas the group performed a one-off show at the Kilburn Gaumont specifically for Jeff Stein to shoot as part of the bio-pic film. It was among the worst concerts they'd ever performed; unrehearsed, mildly intoxicated, nervous and with Keith Moon a serious liability on drums, The Who stumbled along between takes, stopping and starting, a pale shadow of their once staggering selves.

A couple of freak accidents further delayed progress on the new album when sessions resumed in January. John Bundrick, drafted in on keyboards, broke his arm and Pete cut his hand badly. "He had been to visit his parents and they had all had quite a lot to drink," wrote Richard Barnes. "His parents had started an argument and Pete tried to intervene. They were oblivious to him and finally, in a fit of emotion, he smashed his hand through a window. As this only momentarily stopped them, he then rubbed his hand on the broken glass which had the desired effect and his parents stopped their row and rushed him and his bleeding hand off to hospital."

The group re-assembled in March and Glyn Johns moved the sessions to Mickie Most's RAK studios, but Keith was still off form. Roger and John were quite prepared to drop Moon altogether but Pete held firm: after the loss of his friend Kit Lambert he couldn't imagine losing Moon too. "One evening they went for a meal in a restaurant around the corner from RAK," wrote Barnes. "Pete had a talk with him alone. He told him that if he couldn't pull himself together he'd be out of the group."

The pep talk from chairman Townshend had the desired effect and within ten days Keith had completed the drum tracks to everyone's satisfaction. In the end the record was completed with Jon Astley doing most of the production.

Keith Moon performed his last concert with The Who on the Shepperton sound stage in May 1978. Like the Kilburn event the previous December, it was to be filmed for *The Kids Are Alright* but unlike the previous concert, it exploded into the kind of Who performance Jeff Stein needed to complete his movie. After a thunderous version of *Won't Get Fooled Again*, Keith staggered over his drum kit and fell into Pete's waiting arms, and as they embraced, some fans rushed the stage to hug the musicians.

Three months later *Who Are You* was released. Its highlight was the title track, a long, winding song inspired by Pete's Speakeasy encounter with Paul Cook and Steve Jones. Issued as a single, an edited version of the song scampered up the charts in both England and America and this helped to push the album up to Number Two on the billboard charts, the highest position any Who LP ever reached.

This was an ironic triumph, for *Who Are You* was by no means an artistic success. Moon's drumming lacked the fire of earlier recordings and the inclusion of three John Entwistle songs –

the highest proportion he'd ever contributed – stymied any feeling of unity in the material. Many of Pete's songs rely on synthesiser patterns similar to the textures of *Quadrophenia* and Roger Daltrey, who sang an Entwistle song for the first time ever, is often called upon to sing in an operatic style. In this respect he handled the job superbly.

It was, indeed, a *different* Who album but the changes seemed half-hearted, as if Pete knew what he wanted but couldn't quite reach far enough. *Music Must Change*, a drum free jazz track, featured Wes Montgomery-style guitar licks while *Guitar And Pen* resembles an out-take from *The Pirates Of Penzance*. Both ended up sounding pretentious; forced performances unsuitable for The Who.

To promote *Who Are You*, Pete, Roger and Keith flew to America in early August for a series of television, radio and press interviews. No sooner had they arrived than news came through of a death in the entourage: Pete Meaden, the ageless Mod who managed them briefly during 1964, died of a drug overdose on August 7, the verdict suicide. Recently he'd been managing the Steve Gibbons Band in partnership with Bill Curbishley. Pete, who'd helped Meaden out financially over the years, did not conceal his grief.

Most of the American interviews homed in on whether The Who would perform live again and, as always, there was disagreement in the ranks. Pete never wanted to tour again; Roger, Keith and John (who spoke on the phone from England) would "find a way to get Pete back on the road somehow".

"The last three years have been the happiest in my life as far as my family goes," Pete told Rolling Stone. "Also... electric guitar hurts my ears. It's bad to the extent that if I'm subjected to really loud noise for a long time I get a lot of pain. And apparently pain is indicative of further damage."

"I understand what Pete's going through," replied Roger. "And I sympathize with him. I've just got a feeling that if we stop touring now, I know I shall regret it and I know Pete will too."

Back in England, Pete had much to occupy his time. He opened a Meher Baba centre called Oceanic near Richmond, financed a book shop in Richmond called Magic Bus and set up various projects under the name of Eel Pie Ltd. These included recording studios and a book publishing company of which he and Karen were directors. Unfortunately, many of these ventures lost thousands of pounds because the staff appointed were either incompetent or sycophantic.

"I was staggered by the stupidity of some of the people Pete had given key jobs," wrote Richard Barnes. "Many people took advantage of his idealistic good nature; not that they were calculating, but, in the main, they were hopelessly disorganised – someone would quite gladly spend all day in a company car looking for a box of staples.

"The Baba centre evolved just like one of Baba's parables. It became far removed from having any real feeling of love surrounding it... the incongrous combination of recording studio and Baba workshop under one roof was a typical badly thought-out move by Pete. The whole place seemed to be a reflection of his own confused state of mind."

Pete was at home in Twickenham on the afternoon of December 7 when the telephone rang. Jackie Curbishley, Bill's wife and assistant, was on the line and the news she passed on reduced Pete to tears. A few minutes later he called Roger Daltrey in Burwash. Roger picked up the phone himself.

"He's done it," said Pete, his voice choking with emotion.

"Who?" asked Roger.

"Keith".

Keith Moon died from an accidental overdose of the drug Heminevrin which had been prescribed to combat alcoholism. An inquest coroner recorded an open verdict and his body was taken to Golders Green Crematorium where cremation took place on September 11, the same day that Pete issued a statement on behalf of The Who.

"We have lost our great comedian," he wrote, "the supreme melodramatist, the man who apart from being the most unpredictable and spontaneous drummer in rock, would have set himself alight if he thought it would make an audience laugh or jump out of its seats. We have lost our drummer but also our alter-ego. He drove us hard many times but his love for every one of us always ultimately came through.

"The Who? We are more determined than ever to carry on and we want the spirit of the group to which Keith contributed so much to go on, although no human being can ever take his place.

"I have always complained that up until now when I have walked into a pub, someone has slid next to me, nudged me, and said, 'Hey, that Keith Moon, what is he really like?' For the first time in my life I will know what to answer. I wish I didn't."

# CHAPTER TEN

The old Who was gone. So, too, were the expectations of their fans, the same fans whose traditional demands had caused so much grief to Pete Townshend in the past four years. Pete shed many tears for Keith Moon but scarcely a drop for the old Who style. Keith's death settled the issue; change was mandatory.

Two options presented themselves: to end The Who there and then or continue with a new drummer. In the end they chose the latter but Pete made an important provision, albeit one that was never explicitly communicated to the others. From now on The Who would no longer have first pick of his material and neither would he set aside the best songs for the group.

This isn't to say that he would henceforth offer inferior material to The Who (although a strong case could be made out to support this), but that he would write for each successive project – group album or solo album – with what he hoped was equal consistency. Unfortunately for The Who, Pete's creative juices flowed more inventively in the weeks before he recorded solo albums.

Such matters had yet to unfold. In the weeks after Keith's death, many meetings were held and a series of conflicting statements indicated at first that no permanent replacement would be appointed; Roger wanted to use different drummers for different projects and Pete wanted to enlarge the band, bringing in a keyboards player and second guitarist as well as a new drummer.

"We are not tied to being The Who any more," said Pete. "We

could be back for concerts at Christmas with three new musicians." Still Pete was reluctant to tour, though he didn't rule out the possibility of isolated shows. "My days of dragging my body around the world on tour are over. I hate touring."

John Entwistle was the first to propose Kenny Jones as The Who's new drummer and Pete was in agreement. Jones had played on the *Tommy* film soundtrack and was well known to them both since his days in The Small Faces. Roger finally agreed but he was reluctant to admit Jones as a full member; though Roger was voted down, he and Kenny often failed to see eye-to-eye.

"Ironically, Keith's passing was a positive thing," Pete told Chris Welch. "It meant that it was impossible to be bound by Who traditions. It had been a yoke on us – how did we break free of traditions – things we were responsible for? We've always been careful not to use outside musicians on sessions, and we never wanted to get into string sections on stage. I feel now there is a tremendous open door and I feel very excited about the fact that The Who is a well established band with a tremendous history but suddenly we're in the middle of nowhere – a new band.

"People have really got to live with the fact that The Who they knew has gone and that they'll never see it again. During the last couple of years I've been saying I don't want to tour. I've had lots of letters from people saying they respect my decision but some of them also say 'I'm a seventeen-year-old Who fan, I've never had a chance to see the band and I think it stinks. I wanna see you'. But they won't. They've lost the opportunity. Keith IS dead and that particular magic that existed is also dead. Quite whether any part of that will still exist on stage when we got together, I don't really know."

Pete's questions were answered on May 2, 1979, when the New Who were unveiled at London's Rainbow Theatre. Original plans suggested that the first concert by the group since Moon's death would be at the Cannes Film Festival, at Frejus, but in the event the Rainbow show was slotted in at forty-eight hours notice. Many of those present – like the seventeen-year-old who wrote to Pete – were third generation

Who fans, young Mods on Vespa scooters who wore parkas over Italian-styled suits. Mod had made a comeback and the old Who logo, the arrow turned skywards, was as crucial to their identity as closely cropped hair.

The spirit of The Who was far from dead. Augmented by Rabbit Bundrick on keyboards, they played as well as ever, ripping through a fairly predictable set with the hungry enthusiasm of groups far younger than themselves. As agile as ever, Pete leapt high into the air, spun his arm and drop-kicked his way across the stage, charging into the set like a rhino.

A week later the act was repeated at Cannes. The purpose of this trip was to launch The Who's two films and many interviews were given from a boat moored offshore in the Mediterranean. *The Kids Are Alright* served its purpose admirably; a fascinating glimpse through The Who's illustrious past without commentary or subtitles, a cult item for Who fans with the emphasis on humour, destructive stage appearances and anarchic behaviour. *Quadrophenia* was transformed into a story of Mods v Rockers and included as its highlight a fierce running battle between the two cults in the streets of Brighton. Like the original album, though, the point of *Quadrophenia* was lost on audiences outside of England.

During the Cannes interviews Pete reiterated his intention not to tour but his words went unheeded by the rest of the group. The following year's roadwork turned out to be as hectic as any period in The Who's career.

Pete made two solo appearances that summer, one for Rock Against Racism and another for Amnesty International, and in September the five-piece Who went to America for a five night stand at Madison Square Garden in New York. They returned to the States in November for a three week series of concerts in the mid-west and north-east. On December 3 the tour visited Cincinnati's Riverfront Coliseum where, in a stampede to take advantage of the festival seating arrangements, eleven fans died.

The Who themselves were not told about the tragedy until after the concert. Roger Daltrey was for cancelling the remainder of the tour but Pete maintained a stiffer outlook. "If we don't play tomorrow, we'll never play again," he said.

Amid much notoriety, The Who carried on, performing the following night at Buffalo Memorial Auditorium and continuing with the tour as if nothing had changed. In fairness to The Who, the incident could have happened to almost any superstar band, for crowd control is handled in a similar manner at each and every big draw rock concert. Thus, much of the blame was shouldered by the police, the security staff and those employed by the promoter and the Coliseum itself.

Nevertheless The Who, through their agency and management, had obviously given permission for the festival seating arrangements which gave rise to the stampede in the first place, and such seating (actually no seating at all – just standing on the floor at the front of the stage) is an open invitation to unruly behaviour.

In a curious way the Cincinnati deaths made The Who more famous than ever. It made headlines all over the world; Time magazine put The Who on its front cover. At the centre of it all Pete seemed confused, unable to cope with this new burden of responsibility and a delayed shock reaction set in. The eventual outcome was to set off another period of intense depression, one in which he was to sink lower than at any other period of his life.

The clearest indication of his muddled state came in an interview with Greil Marcus of Rolling Stone magazine which took place in San Francisco the following April and centred on the Cincinnati incident. Pete has since regretted the interview but, at the time, he appeared less recriminatory than he ought to have been.

"When we were told what happened at that gig, that eleven kids had died – for a second our guard dropped. Just for a second. Then it was back up again," he said.

"It was fuck it! We're not gonna let a little thing like that stop us. That was the way we had to think. We had to reduce it. We had to reduce it because if we'd actually admitted to ourselves the true significance of the event – not just in terms of rock but the fact that it happened at one of our concerts – we could not have gone on and worked. And we had a tour to do. We're a rock 'n' roll band. You know, we don't fuck around worrying about eleven people dying. We care about it, but there is a particular attitude I call the 'tour armour'."

That statement would seem to indicate that Pete's idealism was a thing of the past, that The Who was now the professional institution that Roger Daltrey and John Entwistle had always wanted it to be. Outvoted in the boardroom, Pete was obliged to tour again and perform the same old set of familiar material with increasing reluctance. And his remarks to Marcus only aggravated an already sore point.

"We actually left the States – I know Roger and I had a long conversation about it – with an incredible feeling of, without being mordant about it, of love for the American people. Everybody had been so positive and supportive and understanding – even to the point where people would come up to me and say, 'We know it wasn't your fault.' And to some extent it *was* our fault... there was a great share of responsibility there, and people were so willing to – not so much forgive, but firstly to get us back into shape, so that perhaps it was possible for us to behave in a truly realistic, responsive way about the whole thing.

"I think only time will tell. If I could dare say it, I'd say that Cincinnati was a very, very positive event for The Who. I think it changed the way we feel about people. It's changed the way we feel about our audience.

"I watched Roger Daltrey cry his eyes out after that show. I didn't but he did. But now, whenever a fucking journalist asks you about Cincinnati, they expect you to come up with a fucking theatrical tear in your eye! You know: 'Have you got anything to say about Cincinnati?'. 'Oh, we were deeply moved, terrible tragedy, the horror, loss of life, aaarrrghhh...'. What do you do? We did all the things we thought were right at the time: sent flowers to the fucking funerals. All... wasted. I think when people are dead, they're dead."

Pete's cynical attitude seemed unforgivable and when the interview was published the backlash was perfectly understandable. The families of the bereaved were justifiably shocked and refused a hitherto agreed settlement with The Who. The matter is still being dealt with in the American courts and Pete has apologised publicly for the remarks he made. (He told Dave Marsh: "(It was)... sensationally framed, without vocal inflections; it actually looks like I mean what I'm saying, or at least that I believe what I'm saying is worth saying. When I spoke to Greil Marcus, I was sarcastic and, I thought, self-detrimental about the group's bloody-minded determination to carry on after the tragedy. I was simply to illustrate how absurd show business thinking is. It didn't come off and hurt the feelings of the relatives.")

Towards the end of 1979 Pete signed a solo record deal with Atlantic and thus committed himself to recording three non-Who albums over the next six years. Around the same time the group signed a new American deal with Warner Brothers, said to be worth around twelve million dollars.

The first of Pete's solo albums under the new deal was completed in the early months of 1980. Effectively, it was his first genuine solo work (*Who Came First* was really a tribute to Meher Baba and *Rough Mix* was a duet with Ronnie Lane) and producer Chris Thomas coaxed Pete to give of his all, especially on the vocals. Titled *Empty Glass*, it was a fine collection of songs – several of them would have been suitable for The Who – and a justifiable commercial success.

"If I was really going to do a solo album deal properly, the only way I could do it was to take the best of any material I had at a particular time, rather than knock together solo projects based on material that The Who had rejected," he told Charles Shaar Murray when the album was released in April. "So my album – though I was able to take a lot more risks than The Who would – could have been a Who album if we'd been recording at the time.

"I just decided to write – to write straight from the hip – and offer everything to the project that's going, not earmark stuff. I don't want to deny myself all the Who-type material."

*Empty Glass* was a very personal album (it was dedicated to Karen and his two daughters) on which Pete's regular themes are reiterated: fear of ageing, lost ideals and, in a track called *Jools And Jim*, angst towards the pop media. *Let My Love Open*

*The Door*, a light and catchy pop song, was a successful hit single and the album reached Number Eight in the American Billboard charts.

But the success of *Empty Glass* did little to curb the cycle of depression that Pete was experiencing in 1980. It's title track was a clear admission that his life was in a mess. He'd moved out of the family home in Twickenham and was living at a flat in Chelsea's Kings Road and, when we wasn't recording, his night-time activities incorporated a round of clubs where he drank like a fish, indulged in drugs for the first time since the sixties, and generally drew attention to his empty existence.

He'd ended 1979 with an appearance with The Who at the concerts for Kampuchea at London's Hammersmith Odeon and, on the final night, appeared with Paul McCartney's Rockestra, an all-star aggregation of rock celebrities. Much to McCartney's chagrin Pete was the only member who refused to wear the regulation gold lamé jacket but up on stage he appeared dishevelled, his unkempt hair a tangled mess, baggy trousers bunched at his ankles, swaying drunkenly as if to taunt the prim and proper ex-Beatle.

Neither did his appearance improve on the series of American concerts that followed in the New Year. His playing, too, was erratic. "Occasionally he would play brilliantly... more often, however, Pete would be so out of it on stage that he would start to wander off on his own, jamming away at the end of numbers that the other three had thought had finished," wrote Richard Barnes.

Off stage Pete was living in the room of a thousand identities. His drink and drug habits worsened, he'd talk for hours to anyone who'd listen and he'd stay awake all night after downing a handful of amphetamines. "One night he spoke for hours to some fans who couldn't believe their luck at getting backstage and having Pete talk with them," wrote Barnes. "Eventually even they were exhausted by him and left After talking about everything to everybody, there was nobody remaining as it was about three o'clock in the morning... but Pete ended up talking for another hour to the cleaners."

At a show in Austria which preceded the US tour, Pete had

wandered off on his own to be eventually discovered fast asleep in a bear pit at the local zoo. This incident inspired a song called *Cache Cache* which would appear on The Who's next album *Face Dances*.

In hindsight, Pete has admitted that in the period between 1980 and 1981, he was consciously emulating the behaviour of Keith Moon. He took to flying off without warning to New York or Paris where'd check into an expensive hotel, sleep off the previous night's hangover and then embark on another round of nightclubbing. He partied a great deal with David Bowie (and played guitar on a track on Bowie's *Scary Monsters* album), Elton John and The Rolling Stones.

In London he was often to be found at The Venue in Victoria or at the posh Embassy Club where, like many of its patrons, he'd appear with make-up on his eyes. One night he collapsed at the Club For Heroes and was rushed to hospital with a potential heroin overdose.

Not until the middle of 1982 did Pete speak about this unhappy period. "I was living against a lot of principles of Meher Baba that I initially found enriching," he told Chris Salewicz for Time Out magazine. "Meher Baba came down very heavily against drugs, for example. So for a while I pushed him out of my life because I wouldn't live within those principles... I had an intuition that I was going to burn out – had a couple of very close shaves through getting very drunk and irresponsible, and taking things people were giving me when I didn't know what they were."

A long British tour in the early months of 1981 did nothing to ease Pete's depression. Though most of the concerts were performed with the usual Who finesse, a show at the Rainbow Theatre in February was a disaster. Pete drank four bottles of brandy on stage during the set.

"Basically I decided to go out and not play," he told Salewicz. "I was just going to talk until somebody stopped me and knocked me out. I went out and started to talk but the band began to play without me. I don't really remember a thing about it, except that I'm surprised I didn't kill myself."

"I nearly poisoned myself on another occasion when I woke

up in hospital after going down Club For Heroes. I went blue. I think my heart stopped. That was the point when I decided I was going to have to do something about my drinking."

That British tour – in actuality, the longest that The Who have ever undertaken – coincided with the release of *Face Dances*, the first album recorded with Kenny Jones as a member of the group. It was a disappointment and the group themselves admitted as much later. The songs were wordy, the melodies unmemorable and the style several shades lighter than the best Who music.

Though the drumming was unimaginative compared to that of Keith Moon, it would be unfair to blame Kenny Jones for the failure of *Face Dances*. Bill Szymczyk's production was too light and The Who edge, the sharp chord work for which Pete was noted, was nowhere to be heard. Roger Daltrey effected a modern-sounding British accent but seemed unable to identify with the songs and consequently unable to deliver Pete's lyrics with any real conviction. The fault lay fairly and squarely with Townshend's material and the fact that his better songs of the period had already been recorded on *Empty Glass*.

Attempts to play this material live, including the modest hit single *You Better You Bet*, were soon abandoned and The Who found themselves in a schizophrenic situation wherein their live repertoire differed substantially from the music they recorded, not just in content but in form and style. That the old form and style was better appreciated was reflected in their ability to continue selling concert tickets by the hundred thousand.

If these odd circumstances weren't sufficient to push Pete over the edge during 1981, there occurred two further dispiriting events. On April 7, Kit Lambert, his great friend and mentor, died from injuries received in a fall at his mother's home in Fulham. Earlier the same night he'd been involved in a drunken brawl at a gay nightclub in Kensington. Around the same time Pete's accountants informed him that he was five hundred thousand pounds in the red at the bank.

Most of Pete's business interests had come unstuck. Oceanic, the recording studio and Baba centre, was losing money hand over fist; Eel Pie Publishing put out less titles than the staff they employed; the Magic Bus Bookshop in Richmond had had to be sold. "That hurt my pride," Pete told Salewicz. "I don't like failing. But in the context of the fact that I almost failed at the most important thing of all, which is staying alive. I don't mind losing things like that.

"I was caught in an incredible cleft stick: I'd not wanted to blow the money I had on mansions or Rolls-Royces or homes in LA, because I thought it was much better to create jobs or put the money into something which helps other people create, and to accept that this was part of my responsibility. But then I was unable to follow it through, either because I was so fucked up, or distracted, or simply not here because I was on the road with The Who. Also the people I'd appointed to do the work thought there was an endless supply of money. I suddenly realised that after all the sneering I'd done about Apple, the same thing was happening to me – people were spending my money faster than I could earn it."

Pete had an unpleasant meeting at the National Westminster Bank. "I still had an account at the same bank in Ealing Common that I'd opened with my first art school grant cheque when I was sixteen. I had the same bank manager as well. But he was about to retire and was getting very worried about all the money I had outstanding – I think he was worried they were going to take it off his pension.

"He asked me if I'd come over and talk to the area manager. So I went and suddenly realised that behind this nice man is the National Westminster Bank who are rats, and they wanted my bollocks; despite the fact that I'd put every personal penny I had into the company to keep it afloat they wanted more. They wanted my house, they wanted my recording contract, they wanted me to sign with them and they would sign me to my record label. I was quite seriously considering the joys of bankruptcy, to live in Paris and have a peaceful life. But in the end I thought, 'No, I'll beat the bastards at their own game. I'll come back from the dead and make some money'."

Which is, indeed, what has happened, though not without a certain amount of pain and self-discipline.

# CHAPTER ELEVEN

In the midst of his depression, Pete worked fitfully on a second solo album, again with producer Chris Thomas. Thomas was one of many close associates who became alarmed at his behaviour and he warned Pete that his voice was likely to be affected by the drugs he was taking. Pete was persuaded to spend two months alone at his riverside house in Oxfordshire where he pottered around in the garden, rowed on the Thames and curbed the excess, but on his return to London the old lifestyle beckoned.

"After three weeks he was back, coked up to the eyeballs, twitching and shaking, surrounded by the same old sycophants from the chic 'living dead' of clubland," wrote his friend Richard Barnes.

In November 1981 Pete admitted his alcoholism to a doctor and was admitted to a clinic. As well as hypnotherapy, he was given an anti-depressant called Ativan eight times a day; in the evening three sleeping pills calmed him down for the night's sleep. Ativan is addictive and Pete became hooked. On his release he took any drug he could lay his hands on, including heroin, to ease the sensation of *not* being drunk. Often he wasn't quite sure exactly what he was smoking or inhaling through his nostrils.

"Someone would be freebasing, and you'd seen them puff in a bit of burning junk through a straw. And that's *it*. A lot of people don't realise you are going to get addicted to heroin instantly by smoking it," he told Chris Salewicz. "If you snort it you don't get addicted instantly, but if you smoke it you do. It's not as dramatic as sitting at a party and banging it in your arm, but it's the same thing."

Sometime during January of 1982 Pete decided that unlike Pete Meaden, Keith Moon and Kit Lambert, he did not wish to die before he got old. "A month later it dawned on me that I was actually dying, that my macho I-can-do-anything mentality would actually kill me," he said. "It was then that I contacted Meg."

Meg Patterson had already successfully cured Keith Richards and Eric Clapton of heroin addiction. At her San Diego clinic during the early months of 1982, using Neuro-Electric Therapy Stimulation, she cured Pete Townshend. "By the second day I realised I was in the home straight," Pete told the American science magazine Omni. "By the third day I felt feelings of sexual desire... an inner joy... At the high setting (on his NET box) I would sometimes have psychedelic experiences."

This extraordinary cure hinges on a small black box worn on the belt that resembles a Sony Walkman tape player. The box induces a natural bodily substance called endrophine, which a heroin addict fails to produce, by emitting a slight electric current. The NET principle, it is claimed, can reduce the time it takes an addict's body to produce normal levels of endrophine from ten months to ten days.

"Somehow that simple little gadget made me feel whole," said Pete. "If I'm ever raped by a crazy pusher and become hooked again I won't hesitate to call Meg and have my addiction handled in this straightforward, completely technical way."

Pete spent a month in California and on his last day was walking with a friend along the beach when he spotted a jar of white powder that had been washed up by the Pacific waves. Bending down by the water's edge, Pete unscrewed the top, dipped a finger inside and placed a few grains of powder on his tongue. He hesitated; then, with all his might, threw the bottle on to some nearby rocks where it smashed into a hundred tiny pieces. Inside was enough cocaine to satisfy his old habit for months.

"I discovered there was a simple enough, rational explanation for why it was there. The nearby port is one of the biggest smuggling bases for stuff going into Los Angeles. Obviously whoever was taking it in lost their nerve and chucked it into the sea," he said later.

"But I do find it very interesting as an example of my feelings about the way in which the devil operates."

It was a new man who returned to London in the spring of 1982. He did not – and does not – drink any form of alcohol or take drugs of any kind. He was reconciled with Karen and his two daughters. His financial insolvency was partially eradicated by the completion of the second solo album and, by the end of the year, he was a millionaire again thanks to what was billed in America as "The Final Who Tour". Eel Pie Books has been sold to Plexus, another London publishing house, and Pete accepted an associate editorship with yet another publishing concern, Faber and Faber. His only vice seems to the tiny and immensely strong Indian cigarettes he virtually chain smokes.

Released in June, *All The Best Cowboys Have Chinese Eyes* reflected the turmoils of the previous twelve months and, like *Empty Glasses*, contains ambitious music that demands attention despite some obtuse lyrics and mildly pretentious semi-poetical passages. Its opening song, *Stop Hurting People*, is a prayer for re-unification with his wife while *Somebody Saved Me*, tottering on the brink of self pity, emerges as an anthem of gratitude to persons unknown who helped Pete out of the abyss.

It was, by Pete's standards, a largely experimental album and one which his American record company was initially reluctant to release. "Originally I did a series of experiments, basically just rhythm tracks with poetry over the top," he said. "When I took the first tracks to New York and played them for the record company, you would have paid money to have seen their faces.

"They said 'Leave it to the *avant-garde*'. David Bowie was with me at the time and he said I should just go ahead and do it – what do record companies know anyway. But I came back and re-wrote half the album. There's little point in sitting and writing material and getting obsessed with whatever you choose to get obsessed with and then have nobody to listen."

136

Amid the introspection were three catchy pop songs: *Face Dances Part Two*, a single that deserved a higher chart placing than it achieved; *Uniforms*, a song about cults; and *Slit Skirts*, a crisply recorded rocker with an energy that belies its lyrical complexity. Among the musicians Pete used on the album were bass player Tony Butler and drummer Mark Brzezicki who would shortly become the rhythm section of Big Country, one of the UK's most successful new bands of 1983.

With the solo album completed, Pete turned his attention back to The Who. Glyn Johns was brought back for the recording of *It's Hard*, but the quality of the material once again failed to measure up to his solo work. Before recording started there was a band meeting to discuss the problem.

"I sat around with everybody and asked them what they wanted to sing about," Pete told Richard Barnes. "'Tell me and I'll write the songs', I said. It's a piece of piss... I've been writing songs for twenty years." Common ground for subject matter included conservation, the threat of nuclear war and political instability.

"We wanted to do something that was to do with life, that was real and hopefully a little easier to read than some of the songs on the last album which were very obtuse."

The album was recorded and almost completed during May and all of the group were happier with the result than they had been with *Face Dances*. "It wasn't the time it took... it was also the atmosphere," said Pete. "It was almost like we had nothing to lose. I nearly lost everything that I had and so I'm glad to have what I've got. I feel very good about the band just being what they are."

The best track on the record, *Eminence Front*, was the most un-Who like track of all, another of Pete's winding build up songs on which he took lead vocals: it could have been a solo track. Elsewhere, John Entwistle had three numbers – his increased allowance on Who albums is in a direct ratio to Pete's commitment to solo material – and the title track glistened with a spark of their earlier selves.

By the time of its September release, Pete was ready to tour again. Earlier in the year this seemed unlikely and even Roger

Daltrey, much as he loved performing, had been ready to abandon The Who if such a course would cure Pete of his depression. "I was responsible for getting him back on the road after 1978," Roger told Rolling Stone magazine. "And after three tours of America he was a bloody junkie. I felt responsible for that. I was really hard to live with and I just didn't want to do it any more. I mean, I think the world of that guy. I think enough of him to stop The Who."

Roger's offer meant a great deal to Pete. "He was the most vociferous member of the group in saying that he would do anything, give up anything – even give up the group – if it would make me happy," he admitted.

And so, amid much fanfare, The Who toured for a final time. They performed two shows at Birmingham's National Exhibition Centre on September 9 and 10 and kicked off their longest American tour in twelve years at Washington DC on September 22. The Birmingham shows were tight, well balanced and effortlessly professional. Two new songs were included in a set that again stretched back into their illustrious history for the most part, and audiences were treated to the rare sight of seeing Roger Daltrey play guitar alongside Pete. Each show climaxed with John Entwistle singing *Twist And Shout* but no guitars were broken and, as far as Pete was concerned, no alcohol consumed.

In commercial terms, the American tour was the most successful of the group's career. A beer company bought the rights to their name and the group performed in outdoor arenas where audiences approaching six figures sat in miserable weather to watch a show that was repeated identically every night.

"We don't necessarily want to be dependent on one another but we are," Pete told Rolling Stone magazine midway through the tour. "So it doesn't matter whether you walk away from this relationship... it still remains."

It was billed as the "Final Tour" but The Who hedged their bets. Roger and Pete said that there would be more Who records (they're contractually obligated to produce more albums anyway) and perhaps the odd one-off concert but no more tours. John was unhappy with this – as, presumably, was

138

Kenny Jones – and said he would leave them to it and form a new band of his own. Plans for concerts during 1983, rumoured throughout the year, did not materialise. No records by the group or individual members were released at all during 1983, apart from *Scoop*, the collection of demos Pete had recorded at various times over twenty years.

This double album included many unheard Townshend songs alongside more familiar material, and Pete's characteristically laconic liner notes were as interesting and revealing as ever. *Scoop* demonstrated how closely The Who have followed their leader's footsteps over the years, how Pete's rhythm guitar has suggested percussive lines for Keith Moon and how closely Roger has echoed Pete's guide vocals.

With the release of *Scoop*, rumoured likely for release anytime during the past decade, Pete cleared the decks. It had been promised for years and its final arrival came as a thinly disguised full stop.

During the early months of 1983 Pete found himself no longer able to write material suitable for The Who. After almost twenty years as their principal composer, he had finally run out of ideas and the problem was unlikely to be resolved with time. In May Pete informed the rest of the group that he no longer wanted the responsibility of being a part of The Who.

No one took Pete seriously, not at first, and as a result no public announcement was made until December. When it came, it was buried away in the back pages of the bumper Christmas editions that the music press publish once a year. In 1970 the news would have called for banner headlines – "PETE QUITS WHO SHOCK!" – and a sensational front page story. Now it no longer mattered; if Pete Townshend no longer cared about The Who, neither did the rest of the world. "I will not be making any more records with The Who and I will not perform live again, anywhere in the world, with The Who," began Pete's written statement and all speculation henceforth ceased. (Among the speculators had been Roger Daltrey who, in a TV interview ten days earlier, suggested that The Who was still a going concern).

"In the first three months of this year, I wrote songs for the next contracted Who album, and I realised after only a short time that they weren't suitable for The Who," Pete's statement continued. "In March I informed the other members of the band and our manager that I was in difficulties. Several ideas were thrown around but none helped me.

"Therefore in May, I met with the band again and to tell them that I had decided to quit, leaving The Who ball in their court. I did nothing more until September when I felt that, out of courtesy, I should explain my problem to the chairman of Warner Bros USA, Mo Ostin. He was sympathetic and made several suggestions, none of which helped me.

"On December 7 we received Warner Brothers' notice of termination of contract. I feel sad that I cannot honour our commitment to Warners – and that many of our fans, both old and new, will be upset after being exposed to rumours that we were recording all this year. The fact is we didn't even book studio time.

"My solo deal with Atco will continue, and I hope to record an album next year. I wish Roger, John and Kenny the best of luck with their future work and thank them for their patience."

Thus ended The Who. Hearing the news was like hearing of the death of a close friend who'd suffered from a terminal illness for some time. It was still a shock, albeit an expected one; the career of rock's finest live performers terminated because the band's leader, realising that its brain was dead, now elected to cut off the life-support system.

The Who had clearly become a millstone around Pete's neck. Asked what The Who meant to him during the final US tour, he replied with typical candour, "Around one million dollars a year." Twenty years of idealism were shattered in a single sentence.

Predicting Townshend's future is hazardous. Two years ago that future looked bleak, barely existent, yet today his mental and physical health is as sound as ever. He is the longest serving, most honest man in rock; eternally idealistic, if occasionally foolish; for the most part incorruptable and always entertaining. He did not, as he once hoped, die before he got old and for that one lie, the greatest in rock, we should be profoundly grateful.

140

# CHRONOLOGY

1917            Birth of Clifford Blandford Townshend in
                Brentford, West London.

1924            Birth of Betty Veronica Dennis in Marylebone,
                London.

1935            Birth of Christopher 'Kit' Lambert in
                Knightsbridge, London.

1944            Marriage of Clifford Townshend and Betty
                Dennis at Pontypool Register Office, South
                Wales.

19th May, 1945  Birth of Peter Dennis Blandford Townshend at
                Central Middlesex Hospital, Chiswick, West
                London.

1956            PT enters Acton County Grammar School;
                outsize nose inspires class ridicule; vows to
                'show 'em one day'.

Summer 1957     PT sees Bill Haley film *Rock Around The Clock*
                several times during extended holiday on Isle of
                Man.

Christmas 1957  PT receives first guitar as Christmas present
                from maternal grandmother.

1958            PT abandons guitar in frustration and turns to
                banjo.

1959            PT plays banjo with The Confederates,
                schoolboy traditional jazz band; befriends John
                Entwistle, budding trumpeter and fellow pupil
                at Acton CGS.

| 1960 | PT acquires second guitar for three pounds from mother's antique shop; practises night and day; performs casually with The Aristocrats (aka The Scorpions) with John Entwistle on newly-acquired homemade bass guitar. |
|---|---|
| 1961 | PT leaves Acton County Grammar School to take up four year graphic design course at Ealing Art College; relocates from parents' Ealing home to shared flat close to college grounds; follows Entwistle's footsteps in joining The Detours, local quintet led by singer/guitarist Roger Daltrey; defers to Daltrey on group decisions. |
| 1962 | PT becomes sole Detours guitarist after personnel shuffle; writes first song (*It Was You*) and exerts influence over choice of material performed; introduced to imported American jazz, blues and r&b (and marijuana) by American college buddy Tom Wright; impressed by *avant garde* musician Andy "Thunderclap" Newman, auto-destructive artist Gustav Metzke and pop art college curriculum. |
| 1963 | Detours contracted to West London agency and perform regularly in pubs and clubs as material becomes more sophisticated; PT much influenced by Rolling Stones and Johnny Kidd's guitarist Mick Green; Detours re-christened The Who. |
| Spring 1964 | Keith Moon replaces original Detours/Who drummer Doug Sandom. |

| | |
|---|---|
| May 1964 | Arch Mod Pete Meaden becomes Who co-manager and publicist; group's name changed to The High Numbers and appropriate Mod image adopted. |
| June 1964 | The High Numbers appear live at The Scene Club, a popular gathering place for Mods in London's West End. |
| July 1964 | *I'm The Face/Zoot Suit*, the first and only release by The High Numbers, released into a vacuum. |
| September 1964 | Kit Lambert and Chris Stamp oust Pete Meaden as managers of The High Numbers; group's name reverts back to The Who; PT smashes first guitar following accident and temper tantrum at Railway Hotel, Harrow. |
| November 1964 | The Who begin sixteen week residency at London's Marquee Club; PT smashes more guitars and writes more songs (including *I Can't Explain* and *The Kids Are Alright*) under the encouraging eye of Kit Lambert in whose Belgravia flat he now resides; first critical mentions of The Who appear in the London music press. |
| December 1964 | Lambert and Stamp sign production deal with American expatriate record producer Shel Talmy who secures worldwide record deal with American Decca; in the UK their records will appear on Brunswick label. |
| January 1965 | *I Can't Explain* released; The Who appear on Ready, Steady, Go! |

| | |
|---|---|
| April 1965 | The Who make their first appearance on Top Of The Pops; *I Can't Explain* reaches Number Nine in UK charts. |
| May 1965 | *Anyway, Anyhow, Anywhere* (10) released and subsequently chosen as Ready, Steady, Go! theme tune. |
| June 1965 | The Who perform in Paris on their first trip abroad. |
| August 1965 | The Who startle fans with their destructive show at The Richmond Jazz and Blues Festival. |
| September 1965 | Backstage squabbles mar tour of Holland, Denmark and Sweden. |
| October 1965 | Roger is fired from The Who but re-instated after mediation by Kit Lambert; alternative proposals for PT include his leading the remaining trio or fronting new group with Paddy, Klaus and Gibson, trio managed by Brian Epstein. |
| November 1965 | *My Generation* (2) released. |
| December 1965 | *My Generation* LP released. |
| February 1966 | The Who join package tour with The Fortunes, The Merseybeats, The Graham Bond Organisation and Screaming Lord Sutch. |
| March 1966 | *Substitute* (PT's first production) released and reaches number five in UK charts after considerable delay caused by split with Shel Talmy; following lawsuit and subsequent out-of-court settlement, The Who's records will appear .. |

on the Reaction label in UK; The Who appear on cover of Sunday Observer Magazine.

April 1966 — The Who make their second visit to France; also join package tour with The Spencer Davis Group and The Merseybeats.

May 1966 — PT in M1 car crash following show at Lincoln City Football Ground; erroneous reportage leads to rumour that Roger Daltrey is dead.

June 1966 — Tour of Denmark, Sweden and Finland.

July 1966 — Amid other UK performances The Who appear at the Windsor Jazz and Blues Festival.

August 1966 — *I'm A Boy* (2) (Kit Lambert's first production) released along with single edit of *The Kids Are Alright* (31); sessions for *A Quick One* commence.

October 1966 — Six day visit to Sweden and Denmark; *Ready, Steady, Who!* TV show aired.

November 1966 *Ready, Steady, Who!* EP released along with single of *La La La Lies*; latter fails to chart.

December 1966 *A Quick One* LP released; *Happy Jack* (3) released; final appearance on Ready, Steady, Go!

January 1967 — The Who appear at London's Savile Theatre with Jimi Hendrix on the same bill.

February 1967 — The Who perform in Italy for the first time.

March 1967 — The Who visit America for the first time and perform a week of concerts (five a day) at The Brooklyn Theatre in New York presented by DJ Murray The K; *Happy Jack* becomes first US hit.

| | |
|---|---|
| April 1967 | German tour with John's Children; *Pictures Of Lily* (4), their first release on Lambert and Stamp's newly-formed Track label, released. |
| June 1967 | Irish tour; Monterey Festival appearance in California; *The Last Time/Under My Thumb* (44) recorded and released in sympathy with Rolling Stones' drug sentences. |
| July/ August 1967 | Eight week US tour supporting Herman's Hermits. |
| October 1967 | *I Can See For Miles* (10) released. |
| November 1967 | Month long US tour supporting The Animals; *The Who Sell Out* LP released; PT, having forsaken drugs, is introduced to the teachings of Indian mystic Meher Baba and becomes a "Baba lover". |
| January 1968 | Disastrous Australian tour with The Small Faces, Manfred Mann and John Walker of The Walker Brothers. |
| February/ March/ April 1968 | Ten week US tour headlining for the first time and including three nights at San Francisco's Fillmore West and two at New York's Fillmore East. |
| May 1968 | PT marries Karen Astley at Didcot Register Office; they make their home alongside the River Thames at Twickenham. |
| June 1968 | *Dogs* (25) released. |
| July/ August 1968 .. | Seven week US tour; PT stops smashing guitars and outlines ideas and plot for *Tommy* in |

146

lengthy interview with Jann Wenner for Rolling Stone magazine.

September 1968 *Magic Bus* (26) released.

October/ November 1968 Six week UK tour punctuated by recording sessions for *Tommy*; *Direct Hits* compilation LP released.

December 1968 The Who take part in Rolling Stone "Rock 'n' Roll Circus" TV show which is never aired.

January/ February 1969 UK dates interspersed with further *Tommy* recording sessions.

March 1969 *Pinball Wizard* (4) released; The Who rehearse *Tommy* stage show.

May 1969 *Tommy* previewed live before press at Ronnie Scott's Club in London; *Tommy* double LP released; hailed by critics as masterpiece or sacrilege; Thunderclap Newman's *Something In The Air* (1), produced by PT, released; six week US tour opens in New York.

August 1969 The Who perform at the Woodstock Festival in USA, and at the Isle Of Wight Festival.

October/ November 1969 Six week US tour to wild acclaim which henceforth occurs at each and every Who concert.

December 1969 The Who perform *Tommy* at The Covent Garden Opera House in London.

January 1970 The Who tour European opera houses performing *Tommy* to a mixture of rock fans and cultural intelligentsia.

February 1970    *Live At Leeds* LP recorded during concert at
                 Leeds University; *The Seeker* (19) released; *Happy
                 Birthday*, PT's first private Meher Baba LP,
                 released.

May 1970         *Live At Leeds* LP released.

June/            Six week US tour includes supposed final
July 1970        performance of *Tommy* at New York's
                 Metropolitan Opera House; *Summertime Blues*
                 (38) released.

August 1970      The Who perform at the Isle of Wight Festival.

October 1970     Extensive UK tour.

February 1971    The Who perform at London's Old Vic Theatre
                 in the hope of realising PT's "Lifehouse"
                 concept: the experiment is unsuccessful.

March/           "Lifehouse/Who's Next" songs recorded at
April 1971       Stargroves, Mick Jagger's country home, and
                 Olympic Studios in Barnes with Glyn Johns as
                 producer.

June 1971        *Won't Get Fooled Again* (9) released.

July 1971        *Who's Next* LP released; Six week US tour opens
                 at Forest Hills Tennis Stadium in New York.

September 1971   The Who perform before thirty-five thousand
                 fans at the Oval Cricket Ground in Kennington,
                 London, as preface to four week UK tour.

October 1971     The Who open London's Rainbow Theatre with
                 a three night run.

November/        Six week US tour opens in Charlotte, North
December 1971     Carolina; *Meaty, Beaty, Big And Bouncy*
..

compilation LP released: *Let's See Action* (16) released.

February/ PT undertakes pilgrimage to tomb of Meher
March 1972 Baba in India; *I Am*, PT's second private Meher
Baba LP, issued: ten years later The Who appear
on the cover of The Observer Magazine.

June 1972 *Join Together* (9) released.

August 1972 European tour visits Germany, Holland, France
and Italy.

October 1972 *Who Came First*, PT's first general issue solo LP,
released as tribute to Meher Baba.

November 1972 *Relay* (21) released.

January 1973 PT appears on stage with Eric Clapton's *ad hoc*
comeback band at London's Rainbow Theatre, a
concert he helped organise.

March/April/ *Quadrophenia* recorded at The Who's newly-
May 1973 acquired Rampart Studios in Battersea.

September 1973 *5.15* (20) released.

November 1973 *Quadrophenia* double LP released; unsatisfactory
UK tour spotlights *Quadrophenia*; six week US
*Quadrophenia* tour opens with Keith Moon
collapsing during performance in San Francisco.

December 1973 PT, along with rest of Who entourage, spend
night in gaol following destructive outbreak in
Montreal Hotel suite; four *Quadrophenia* shows
at London's Edmonton Sundown Theatre.

February 1974 *Quadrophenia* shows abandoned after brief
..

French tour.

March 1974    PT commences re-recording *Tommy* for film soundtrack with questionable enthusiasm.

April 1974    PT appears in first ever public solo performance at London's Roundhouse; shooting of *Tommy* film starts at Southsea.

May 1974    The Who perform before fifty thousand fans at Charlton Football Ground in London; PT dissatisfied with show.

June 1974    The Who perform four concerts at New York's Madison Square Garden; PT horrified with shows.

Remainder 1974 Depressed at future Who prospects, PT labours and early 1975    over *Tommy* soundtrack and songs for next Who LP: *Odds And Sods* released (October).

March 1975    *Tommy* film premiered in New York and Los Angeles.

May 1975    PT criticises The Who (and many others) in controversial NME interview; *Who By Numbers* recorded at Rampart Studios.

June 1975    Roger Daltrey criticises PT in NME rejoinder.

October 1975    *Who By Numbers* LP released; mutually satisfying twelve concert UK tour opens in Stafford.

November 1975 Equally satisfying month long US tour opens in Texas.

December 1975 Three Christmas concerts at London's Hammersmith Odeon apparently cement Who solidarity.

January 1976    *Squeeze Box* (10) – a by now rare appearance in the singles chart – released.

March 1976    Two Paris shows followed by month long Who US tour; Keith Moon passes out during opening night in Boston.

May/
June 1976    Brief UK tour visits football stadiums at Charlton, Swansea and Glasgow; Bill Curbishley officially takes over from Kit Lambert and Chris Stamp as Who manager.

August 1976    The Who perform four US stadium concerts.

September 1976 *The Story Of The Who* compilation LP released.

October 1976    US and Canadian Who tour marks Keith Moon's last appearances in North America; *Substitute* (7) re-released.

March 1977    PT confronts Sex Pistols at London's Speakeasy Club.

September 1977 *Rough Mix*, PT's LP with Ronnie Lane, released; concurrent interviews offer little promise of renewed Who activity.

December 1977 The Who perform at Kilburn State Theatre for a sequence in their upcoming bio-pic *The Kids Are Alright*.

Early 1978    Erratic progress is made during sessions for next Who LP.

May 1978    The Who perform before an invited audience at Shepperton Studios in a further sequence for *The Kids Are Alright*; Keith Moon's final Who appearance.

| | |
|---|---|
| July 1978 | *Who Are You* (18) released. |
| August 1978 | *Who Are You* LP released. |
| September 1978 | Keith Moon dies in Mayfair flat. |
| January 1979 | Kenny Jones confirmed as new Who drummer. |
| April 1979 | *Long Live Rock* (48) released. |
| May 1979 | New look Who, with Kenny Jones and John 'Rabbit' Bundrick on keyboards, perform at London's Rainbow Theatre; two Who films *The Kids Are Alright* and *Quadrophenia* premiered at Cannes Film Festival; four concerts performed in France. |
| June 1979 | *The Kids Are Alright* double LP released; PT appears solo in Amnesty International charity concert in London. |
| July 1979 | PT leads *ad hoc* band at Rock Against Racism concert in London. |
| September 1979 | *Quadrophenia* film soundtrack released; new look Who perform five nights at New York's Madison Square Garden. |
| December 1979 | Month long US tour includes concert at Cincinnati Riverfront Coliseum where eleven fans are killed during rush to get inside arena; The Who perform at the Concerts For Kampuchea at London's Hammersmith Odeon and PT appears with Paul McCartney's Rockestra. |
| March 1980 | Short European tour visits Germany and Austria. |

| April 1980 | Five week US tour opens in Vancouver; *Empty Glass*, first PT solo album since *Who Came First*, released. |
| June 1980 | Month long US tour opens in San Diego; *Let My Love Open The Door* (46), PT solo single released. |
| January 1981 | Twenty-two date UK tour opens in Sheffield and includes unsatisfactory concert at London's Rainbow Theatre. |
| February 1981 | *You Better You Bet* (9) released; The Who make rare appearance on Top Of The Pops. |
| March 1981 | Lengthy European tour cancelled at PT's behest; *Face Dances* LP released. |
| April 1981 | Kit Lambert, ex-Who manager and long time associate of PT, dies in London. |
| May 1981 | *Don't Let Go The Coat* released: fails to chart. |
| Winter 1981 | PT undergoes treatment for alcoholism. |
| January 1982 | PT undergoes treatment for heroin addiction at Meg Patterson's clinic in California. |
| June 1982 | *All The Best Cowboys Have Chinese Eyes*, PT's third solo album, released. |
| September 1982 | *It's Hard* LP released; two concerts at Birmingham's National Exhibition Centre preface lucrative two month US and Canadian tour; PT and Daltrey state that this will be The Who's final concert tour but do not dismiss the possibility of future albums and one-off shows. |
| December 1983 | PT announces that he will no longer make |

..

records or perform with The Who anywhere in the world.

NB: Figures in brackets after singles indicate highest UK chart position reached.

# APPENDIX I

This is an alphabetical listing of one hundred and seventy-nine songs written by Pete Townshend, some recorded by The Who, some recorded by Pete alone, and a handful of others. In certain cases songs have been recorded by both The Who and by Pete as a solo performer, or simply demoed by Pete and made available to the public. It is, of course, assumed that every Who song has at one time been demoed by Pete alone.

*Acid Queen*
From *Tommy* LP (Track 613 013/4, released May 1969); also appears on *Tommy* by The London Symphony Orchestra (ODE SP 88001, released October 1972) sung by Merry Clayton and on *Tommy* film soundtrack LP (Polydor 9502, released March 1975) sung by Tina Turner; also on *Story* LP. Originally written as an anti-drug song but misconstrued by, among others, Vice-President of the USA Spiro Agnew.

*A Little Is Enough*
From *Empty Glass* LP (ATCO 50699, released April 1980).

*A Man Is A Man*
From *It's Hard* LP (Polydor WHOD 5066, released September 1982); also "B" side of *Athena* single.

*Amazing Journey*
From *Tommy* LP; also appears on *Tommy* by LSO sung by Pete and on *Tommy* soundtrack also sung by Pete; also on *Story* LP. The first written to be included in *Tommy*.

*And I Moved*
From *Empty Glass* LP.

*Anyway, Anyhow, Anywhere*
The Who's second single (Brunswick 05935, released May 1965);
..

also appears on *Meaty Beaty Big And Bouncy* (Track 2406 006, released October 1971). A joint writing credit with Roger Daltrey though Pete is understood to have contributed the lion's share. Reached Number Ten in UK charts; chosen as theme tune for Ready Steady Go!

### Athena
From *It's Hard* LP; also a single (Polydor WHO6, released September 1982) and concurrent picture single and 12" single.

### Baba O'Riley
From *Who's Next* LP (Track 2408 102, released July 1971); also appears on *The Story Of The Who* LP (Polydor 2683 069, released September 1976) and on *The Kids Are Alright* soundtrack (Polydor 2675 179, released June 1979) performed live. A song written for the aborted Lifehouse project and often performed in concert.

### Bargain
From *Who's Next* LP; also appears on *Story* and as demo on *Scoop* (ATCO 79 0063 1, released May, 1983).
A song about "losing one's ego as a devotee of Meher Baba"; written for Lifehouse.
The demo version is master quality and uncannily similar to the version on *Who's Next*.

### (To) Barney Kessell
From *Scoop*.
Solo jazz guitar instrumental recording during *Who By Numbers* demo sessions in 1975.

### Behind Blue Eyes
From *Who's Next*; also appears on *Story* LP.
Written for Lifehouse and often performed in concert.

### Bell Boy
From *Quadrophenia* LP (Track 2657 013, released November
..

1973); also appears on *Quadrophenia* film soundtrack LP (Polydor 2625 037, released September 1979). Alternate verses sung by Keith Moon.

**Blue Red And Grey**
From *Who By Numbers* LP (Polydor 2490 129, released October 1975).
Virtually a solo song by Pete.

**Body Language**
From *Scoop*.
Written for *Chinese Eyes* LP but only demoed.

**Brrr**
From *Scoop*.
Instrumental demo recorded at Twickenham.

**Cache Cache**
From *Face Dances* (Polydor 2302 106 WHOD 5037, released March 1981); also appears as demo on *Scoop*.

**Call Me Lightning**
"B" side of *Dogs* single; also appears on *Direct Hits* LP (Track 612 006, released November 1968)

**Can't Reach You**
From *Who Sell Out* LP (Track 612 002, released November 1967).
One of the first songs Pete wrote on piano.

**Cat's In The Cupboard**
From *Empty Glasses* LP.

**Champagne**
From *Tommy* soundtrack LP sung by Ann-Margret and Roger Daltrey. Written for the film and not included on The Who's *Tommy* LP.

**Christmas**
From *Tommy* LP; also on *Tommy* by LSO sung by Steve
Winwood and Roger Daltrey and on *Tommy* soundtrack LP
sung by Ann-Margret, Oliver Reed and Alison Dowling.

**Circles**
First "B" side of *Substitute* single; also appears on *Ready Steady
Who!* EP (Reaction 592001, released November 1966) and as a
demo on *Scoop*.
Demo recorded in Belgravia in 1965.
(The *Ready Steady Who!* EP is a prize collectors' item, selling for
up to one hundred pounds in 1983).

**Classified**
"B" side of *Let My Love Open The Door* single; also appears on
*Revelation*, an anthology of music for Glastonbury Fayre,
released 1972.

**Communication**
From *Chinese Eyes* LP (ATCO K50889, released June 1982).

**Cookin'**
From *Scoop* LP.

**Cook's County**
From *It's Hard* LP.

**Content**
From Pete's first solo LP *Who Came First* (Track 2408 201,
released October 1972).

**Cry If You Want**
From *It's Hard* LP.

**Cut My Hair**
From *Quadrophenia* LP.

**Daily Records**
From *Face Dances* LP (Polydor 2302 106 WHOD 5037, released March 1981).

**Day Of Silence**
Unreleased.
Written on July 10, 1970 – the date in the year when followers of Meher Baba observe a day of silence.

**Did You Steal My Money?**
From *Face Dances* LP.

**Dirty Jobs**
From *Quadrophenia* LP.

**Dirty Water**
From *Scoop* LP.
Recorded at AIR studios in central London during demo sessions for *Face Dances* LP but left off album.

**Disguises**
From *Ready Steady Who!* EP.

**Doctor Jimmy**
From *Quadrophenia*; also on *Quadrophenia* soundtrack LP.

**Dogs**
Single (Track 604 023, released June 1968); also appears on *Direct Hits* LP.
Reached Number Twenty-five in UK charts.

**Don't Know Myself**
"B" side of *Won't Get Fooled Again* single.

**Don't Leg Go The Coat**
From *Face Dances* LP.

**Don't Look Away**
From *A Quick One* LP.

**Do You Think It's Alright?**
From *Tommy* LP; also appears on *Tommy* by LSO sung by
Maggie Bell and Steve Winwood and on *Tommy* soundtrack LP
sung by Ann-Margret and Oliver Reed: also on *Story* LP.

**Dreaming From The Waist**
From *Who By Numbers* LP.

**Drowned**
From *Quadrophenia*

**Early Morning Cold Taxi?**
An out-take from *Who Sell Out*. Remains unreleased.

**Eminence Front**
From *It's Hard* LP.
Featured in 1982 concerts, the first occasion since the early days
of The Detours when Roger Daltrey played guitar on stage.

**Empty Glass**
From *Empty Glass* LP.

**Exquisitely Bored**
From *Chinese Eyes*

**Face Dances Part II**
Solo single (ATKO K11734, released May 1982); also appears on
*Chinese Eyes* LP.

**5.15**
Single (Track 2094 115, released September 1973); also from
*Quadrophenia* LP and *Quadrophenia* soundtrack LP.
Reached Number Twenty in UK charts. One of the few songs
from *Quadrophenia* to be retained in concert after initial
*Quadrophenia* tour.

**Four Faces**
From *Quadrophenia* soundtrack LP; one of three songs prepared for the film but not on original album.

**Getting In Tune**
From *Who's Next*.

**Get Out And Stay Out**
From *Quadrophenia* soundtrack LP; one of three songs prepared for the film but not on original album.

**Glow Girl**
From *Odds And Sods* LP (Track 2406 116, released October 1974). Incorporates a coda with lyrics and melody that subsequently appeared as *It's A Boy* on *Tommy* LP.

**Goin' Fishin'**
From *Scoop* LP.

**Going Mobile**
From *Who's Next*.
Contains one of the best guitar solos Pete has ever recorded.

**Gonna Get Ya**
From *Empty Glass* LP.

**The Good's Gone**
From *My Generation* LP (Brunswick LAT 8616, released December 1965).

**Go To The Mirror**
From *Tommy* LP; also on *Tommy* by LSO sung by Roger Daltrey, Steve Winwood and Richard Harris and on *Tommy* soundtrack sung by Jack Nicholson, Ann-Margret and Oliver Reed.

**Greyhound Girl**
Additional "B" side of *Let My Love Open The Door*.

**Guitar And Pen**
From *Who Are You* LP (Polydor 2490 147 WHOD 5004, released August 1978).

**Happy Jack**
Single (Reaction 591010, released December 1966); also appeared on *Story*, *Direct Hits* LP, *Meaty* LP and *Kids* LP. Reached Number Three in UK charts; The Who's first US hit single.

**Heart To Hang On To**
From *Rough Mix*, Pete's joint LP with Ronnie Lane (Polydor 2442 147, released September 1977).

**Helpless Dancer**
From *Quadrophenia* LP; also appears on *Quadrophenia* soundtrack LP.

**How Can You Do It Alone?**
From *Face Dances* LP.

**However Much I Booze**
From *Who By Numbers* LP.

**How Many Friends**
From *Who By Numbers* LP.

**I Am An Animal**
From *Empty Glass* LP.

**I Am The Sea**
From *Quadrophenia* LP; also appears on *Quadrophenia* soundtrack LP.

**I Can See For Miles**
Single (Track 604011, released October 1967); also appears on *Direct Hits*, *Who Sell Out*, *Meaty*, *Story* and *Kids* LPs. Reached Number Ten in UK charts.

***I Can't Explain***
The Who's first single (Brunswick 05926, released January 1965) discounting The High Number's *I'm The Face/Zoot Suit*; also appears on *Meaty* and *Kids* LPs.

***I'm A Boy***
Single (Brunswick 591004, released August 1966); also appears on *Direct Hits*, *Meaty*, *Story* and *Kids* LPs.
Reached Number Two in UK charts.

***Imagine A Man***
From *Who By Numbers* LP.

***I'm Free***
From *Tommy* LP; also on *Tommy* by LSO sung by Roger Daltrey and *Tommy* soundtrack also sung by Roger Daltrey; also on *Story* LP.

***I'm One***
From *Quadrophenia* LP; also on *Quadrophenia* soundtrack LP.

***In A Hand Or A Face***
From *Who By Numbers* LP.

***Initial Machine Experiments***
From *Scoop* LP.
Synthesiser doodling.

***Instant Party***
Second "B" side of *Substitute* single, also "B" side of *A Legal Matter* single.
Alternative title for *Circles*.

***Is It In My Head***
From *Quadrophenia* LP.

***It's A Boy***
From *Tommy* LP; also appears on *Tommy* by LSO sung by Sandy
..

Denny and on *Tommy* soundtrack sung by Pete, Margot Newman and Vicki Brown.

**It's Hard**
From *It's Hard* LP.

**It's Not True**
From *My Generation* LP.

**It Was You**
Unreleased.
The first song written by Pete; demoed by The Detours and recorded by The Naturals and The Fourmost.

**I've Known No War**
From *It's Hard* LP.

**Jaguar**
Instrumental written for *Who Sell Out* but left off album. Remains unreleased.

**Join Together**
Single (Track 2094 102, released June 1972).
Reached Number Nine in UK charts.

**Joker James**
From *Quadrophenia* soundtrack LP; one of three songs prepared for the film but not on original album.

**Jools And Jim**
From *Empty Glass* LP.

**Keep Me Turning**
From *Rough Mix* LP.

**Keep On Working**
From *Empty Glass* LP; also single (ATCO 11609, released November 1980).

164

**The Kids Are Alright**
Single (Brunswick 05965, released August 1966); also appears
on *My Generation* and *Meaty* LPs. Demoed by The High
Numbers.

**La La La Lies**
Single (Brunswick 05968, released November 1966); first
appears on *My Generation* LP. Did not chart.

**A Legal Matter**
Single (Brunswick 05956, released March 1966); first appears on
*My Generation* LP and also on *Meaty* LP.
Reached Number Thirty-two in UK charts.

**Let My Love Open The Door**
Solo single (ATKO K11486, released June 1980); from *Empty
Glass* LP.
Reached Number Forty-six in UK charts.

**Let's See Action**
Single (Track 2094 102, released November 1971).
Reached Number Eighteen in UK charts. Also appears on *Who
Came First* LP as solo (demo plus) song. Written for Lifehouse.

**Little Billy**
From *Odds And Sods*. Written and recorded at the request of The
American Cancer Society for use in a commercial film but never
used in this capacity.

**Long Live Rock**
Single (Polydor 2121 383 WHO 2); also appears (live) on *Kids* LP.
Reached Number Forty-eight in UK charts. Originally sung by
Billy Fury in the film *That'll Be The Day* which featured Keith
Moon.

**Love Ain't For Keeping**
From *Who's Next* LP

**Love Is Coming Down**
From *Who Are You* LP.

**Love Reign O'er Me**
From *Quadrophenia* LP; also appears on *Quadrophenia* soundtrack LP and as demo on *Scoop* LP.

**Mary**
From *Scoop*. Written for Lifehouse.

**Magic Bus**
Single (Track 604024, released September 1968); also on *Live At Leeds*, *Meaty*, *Story* and *Kids* LPs.
Reached Number Twenty-six in UK charts.

**Mary Ann With The Shakey Hand**
From *Who Sell Out* LP; also on *Direct Hits*.

**Melancholia**
From *Scoop* LP.
Written at Ebury Street studio 1968.

**Miracle Cure**
From *Tommy* LP; also on *Tommy* by LSO sung by 'The Chambre Choir' and on *Tommy* soundtrack sung by Simon Townshend (Pete's brother).

**Misunderstood**
From *Rough Mix* LP.

**Mother And Son**
From *Tommy* soundtrack LP sung by Roger Daltrey and Ann-Margret. Additional track written for film but not on original *Tommy* LP.

**Much Too Much**
From *My Generation* LP.

*Music Must Change*
From *Who Are You* LP.

*My Baby Gives It Away*
From *Rough Mix* LP.

*My Generation*
The Who's third single (Brunswick 05944, released November 1965); also appears on *My Generation, Live At Leeds, Meaty, Story* and *Kids* LPs.
Reached Number Two in UK charts and inspired fifteen different cover versions up to 1983.
The Who's best known song, also made available in demo form on flexi-disc given away with the book *Maximum R&B*.

*Naked Eye*
From *Odds And Sods* LP.
Often performed in concert long before release.

*New Song*
From *Who Are You* LP.

*1921*
From *Tommy* LP; also on *Tommy* by LSO sung by Roger Daltrey, Graham Bell, Steve Winwood and Maggie Bell and on *Tommy* soundtrack sung by Oliver Reed and Ann-Margret (re-titled *1951*).

*North Country Girl*
From *Chinese Eyes* LP.

*Now I'm A Farmer*
From *Odds And Sods* LP.
Intended for release on EP that never materialised.

*Our Love Was*
From *Who Sell Out* LP.

**Out In The Street**
From *My Generation* LP.

**Odorono**
From *Who Sell Out* LP.

**Parvardigar**
From *Who Came First* LP.
A Meher Baba prayer set to music by PT.
Written whilst holidaying in the Blackwater Estuary 1971.

**Pictures Of Lily**
Single (Track 604 006, released April 1967); also appears on
*Direct Hits*, *Meaty* and *Story* LPs.
Reached Number Four in UK charts.

**Pinball Wizard**
Single (Track 604 027, released March 1969); from *Tommy* LP,
also on *Tommy* by RSO sung by Rod Stewart and on *Tommy*
soundtrack sung by Elton John; also appears on *Meaty*, *Story*
and *Kids* LPs, on PT solo performance on *The Secret Policeman's
Ball* LP and as flexi-disc demo given away with the book
*Maximum R&B*.
The most performed song from *Tommy*.
Inspired by journalist Nik Cohn, a friend of Pete's, who is a
skilled pinball player.

**Politician**
From *Scoop* LP.
Recorded at Pete's Wardour Street studios in 1967.

**Popular**
From *Scoop* LP.
Written for The Who's *Face Dances* LP but rejected by the group.

**Prelude**
From *Chinese Eyes* LP.

**The Punk And The Godfather**
From *Quadrophenia* LP; also on *Quadrophenia* soundtrack LP.

**Pure And Easy**
From *Odds And Sods*; also solo track on *Who Came First*.
Written for Lifehouse and incorporated into *Song Is Over* and
*Who's Next* LP.

**Put The Money Down**
From *Odds And Sods* LP.

**Quadrophenia**
From *Quadrophenia* LP.

**A Quick One**
From *A Quick One* LP; also on *Kids* LP live.
Six short songs – *Her Man's Been Gone, Crying Town, We Have A
Remedy, Ivor The Engine Driver, Soon Be Home* and *You Are
Forgiven* – segued together into Pete's first mini-opera.

**Rael**
From *Who Sell Out* LP; aka Sparks and Underture.
Written at Pete's Wardour Street studio 1967: originally
intended as a single and later incorporated into *Tommy*.

**The Real Me**
From *Quadrophenia* LP; also appears on *Quadrophenia* soundtrack
LP.

**Recorders**
From *Scoop* LP.
Atmospheric instrumental intended for *Quadrophenia* but never
used.

**Relax**
From *Who Sell Out* LP.

**Relay**
Single (Track 2094 106, released November 1972).
Reached Number Twenty-one in UK charts.

**The Rock**
From *Quadrophenia* LP.

**Rough Boys**
From *Empty Glass* LP; also single (ATCO K11460, released May 1980).

**Rough Mix**
From *Rough Mix* LP.
Instrumental jointly written with Ronnie Lane.

**Run Run Run**
From *A Quick One* LP; also on *Story* LP.

**Sally Simpson**
From *Tommy* LP; also appears on *Tommy* by LSO sung by Pete and on *Tommy* soundtrack sung by Pete and Roger Daltrey.

**Sea And Sand**
From *Quadrophenia* LP.

**The Sea Refuses No River**
From *Chinese Eyes* LP.

**The Seeker**
Single (Track 604 036, released February 1970); also appears on *Meaty* LP.
Reached Number Nineteen in UK charts.

**See Me Feel Me**
From *Tommy* LP; also appears on *Tommy* sung by LSO sung by Roger Daltrey, *Tommy* soundtrack sung by Roger, on *Story* and on *Kids* LPs as well as *Woodstock* live album. A section from this
..

song is also featured on the extended *My Generation* on *Live At Leeds*.

The climax to *Tommy* and, with *Pinball Wizard*, the most performed song from the entire opera: a concert *tour de force*.

**Sensation**
From *Tommy* LP; also from *Tommy* by LSO sung by Roger Daltrey and on *Tommy* soundtrack sung by Roger.

**Sheraton Gibson**
From *Who Came First* LP.

**Sister Disco**
From *Who Are You* LP.

**Slip Kid**
From *Who By Numbers*; also on *Story* LP.

**Slit Skirts**
From *Chinese Eyes* LP.

**Smash The Mirror**
From *Tommy* LP; also on *Tommy* by LSO sung by Maggie Bell and on *Tommy* soundtrack sung by Ann-Margret.

**Somebody Saved Me**
From *Chinese Eyes* LP.

**Song Is Over**
From *Who's Next* LP.
Written for Lifehouse.

**So Sad About Us**
From *A Quick One* LP; also appears as demo on *Scoop*.
Written at Hanwell 1966.

**Sparks**
From *Tommy* LP (see Rael).

**Squeeze Box**
Single (Polydor 2121 275, released January 1976); from *Who By Numbers* LP, also on *Story* LP and as demo on *Scoop*.
Reached Number Ten in UK charts.

**Stardom In Action**
From *Chinese Eyes* LP.

**Stop Hurting People**
From *Chinese Eyes* LP.

**Street In The City**
Single (Polydor 2058 944, released November 1977); from *Rough Mix* LP.

**Substitute**
Single (Reaction 591001, released March 1966); also appears on *Live At Leeds*, *Direct Hits* and *Story* LPs.
Reached Number Five in the UK charts on initial release and Number Seven on re-release in 1976.
Perennial concert favourite (also recorded by The Sex Pistols).

**Sunrise**
From *Who Sell Out* LP.

**Tattoo**
From *Who Sell Out* LP.

**There's A Doctor**
From *Tommy* LP; also on *Tommy* by LSO sung by Steve Winwood and *Tommy* soundtrack sung by Ann-Margret and Oliver Reed.

**They Are All In Love**
From *Who By Numbers* LP.

**Things Have Changed**
From *Scoop* LP. Demo of song written in 1965.

*Tommy Can You Hear Me*
From *Tommy* LP; also on *Tommy* by LSO sung by Maggie Bell
and on *Tommy* soundtrack sung by Ann-Margret.

*Tommy Overture*
From *Tommy* LP; also *Tommy* by LSO and on *Tommy* soundtrack.

*Too Much Of Anything*
From *Odds And Sods*. Written for Lifehouse.

*TV Studio*
From *Tommy* soundtrack LP sung by Ann-Margret and Oliver
Reed. Composed for film score and not included on Who's
*Tommy* LP.

*Underture*
From *Tommy* LP: see Rael.

*Uniforms*
From *Chinese Eyes* LP.

*Vivienne*
Unreleased; written for *Chinese Eyes* but left off at last minute.

*Water*
"B" side of *5.15*.

*We're Not Gonna Take It*
From *Tommy* LP; also on *Tommy* by LSO and *Tommy* soundtrack
both sung by Roger Daltrey; also on *Story* LP.

*Welcome*
From *Tommy* LP; also from *Tommy* by LSO sung by Roger
Daltrey and *Tommy* soundtrack sung by Roger Daltrey, Ann-
Margret and Oliver Reed.

*Who Are You*
Single (Polydor 2121 361 WHO 1, released July 1978) also
..

appears on *Who Are You* LP.
Reached Number Ten in UK charts.

**Why Did I Fall For That**
From *It's Hard* LP.

**Won't Get Fooled Again**
Single (Track 2094 009, released June 1971); also appears on
*Who's Next*, *Story* and *Kids* LPs.
Reached Number Nine in UK charts.

**You Better You Bet**
Single (Polydor 2002 044 WHO 4, released February 1981); also
appears on *Face Dances* LP.

**You Came Back**
From *Scoop* LP.

**You're So Clever**
From *Scoop* LP.
Written for *Empty Glass* but left off.

**Zelda**
From *Scoop* LP.
Written during *Face Dances* sessions but left off.

# BIBLIOGRAPHY

Barnes, Richard.      Mods! London: Eel Pie, 1979.

Barnes, Richard.      The Who: Maximum R&B. London: Eel Pie, 1982.

Charlesworth, Chris.      The Who: The Illustrated Biography. London: Omnibus 1981

Clarke, Steve.      The Who In Their Own Words. London: Omnibus, 1979.

Cohn, Nik.      Awopbopalooboplopbamboom. London: Weidenfeld & Nicholson 1969.

Hanel, Ed.      The Who: The Illustrated Discography. London: Omnibus, 1981.

Kooper, Al and Edmunds.      Backstage Passes. New York: Stein & Day, 1977.

Marsh, Dace.      Before I Get Old: The Story Of The Who. London: Plexus, 1983.

McKnight, Conner & Silver, Caroline.      The Who: Through The Eyes Of Pete Townshend. New York: Scholastic Book Services, 1974.

Spitz, Robert Stephen.      Barefoot In Babylon. New York: Viking, 1979.

Swenson, John.      The Who. London: Star Books, 1981.

Townshend, Pete & Barnes, Richard.      The Story Of Tommy. London: Eel Pie, 1977.

Turner, Steve (Ed).      A Decade Of The Who. London: Fabulous Music Ltd, 1977.

Waterman, Ivan.      Keith Moon: The Life And Death Of A Rock Legend. London: Arrow, 1979.

Additional research taken from interviews previously published in Rolling Stone, Melody Maker, New Musical Express, Sounds, New Yorker, Rave, International Times, Trouser Press.

The author is grateful to Chris Allen, Chris Welch, Michael Watts, Dave Marsh and Ed Hanel for their help in research.

# THE BEST IN ROCK 'N' ROLL READING
Bestselling rock references

## A-Z OF ROCK SINGERS
by John Tobler

The third volume in the highly acclaimed A-Z of Rock reference series, this book turns the spotlight onto the greatest singers in the first 25 years of rock 'n' roll. Over 250 singers whose distinctive styles, songs and personalities stand out as landmarks of rock history are profiled. Presented in encyclopedic form, each entry contains career background, an assessment of the singer's best work and selected discographies.

128 pages: 60 black/white photos. 8 pages of colour. Selected discographies.
ISBN: 0 86276 139 5 p/b

## A-Z OF ROCK GUITARISTS
by Chris Charlesworth

A companion in the A-Z of Rock reference series, this book brings together the techniques and styles, personalities, classic cuts and performances of over 200 of the world's greatest rock guitarists and bass players.

128 pages: 120 black/white photos. 8 pages of colour. Index and select discographies.
ISBN: 0 86276 080 1 p/b

## A-Z OF ROCK DRUMMERS
by Harry Shapiro

Part of the popular A-Z of Rock reference series, this book focuses on the over 200 drummers who have given the beat to rock 'n' roll from the sixties to the present, from the legendary Ginger Baker to Stewart Copeland of the Police.

128 pages: 120 black/white photos and 8 pages of colour. Index and select discographies.
ISBN: 0 86276 084 4 p/b

## ROCK HERITAGE: THE SIXTIES
by Chris Charlesworth

The first volume in a trilogy on the history of rock 'n' roll, this book features a 20,000-word commentary on international developments of the most tumultuous decade in pop music, portraits of the musicians, songwriters and industry personalities in the vanguard of the rock revolution, a ten-year chronology, and a comprehensive survey of the charts, concerts, festivals and songs that were the sixties.

160 pages: 70 black/white photos. 16 pages colour. Select discography.
ISBN: 0 86276 131 X p/b

## THE PERFECT COLLECTION
Edited by Tom Hibbert

The ultimate rock list book – 200 albums to have on a desert island.

96 pages: 100 black/white photos.
ISBN: 0 86276 105 0 p/b

## RARE RECORDS
by Tom Hibbert

In-depth information on little known masterpieces and the record collecting trade. A must for all collectors.

128 pages: 50 colour and black/white photos.
ISBN: 0 86276 047 X p/b